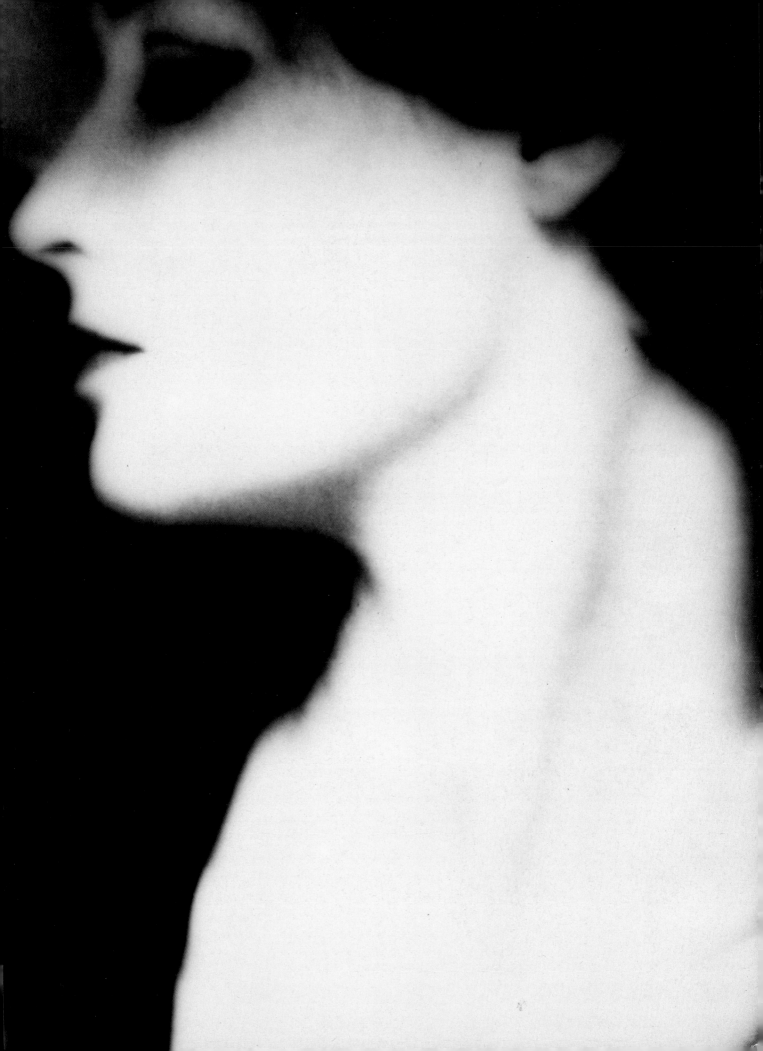

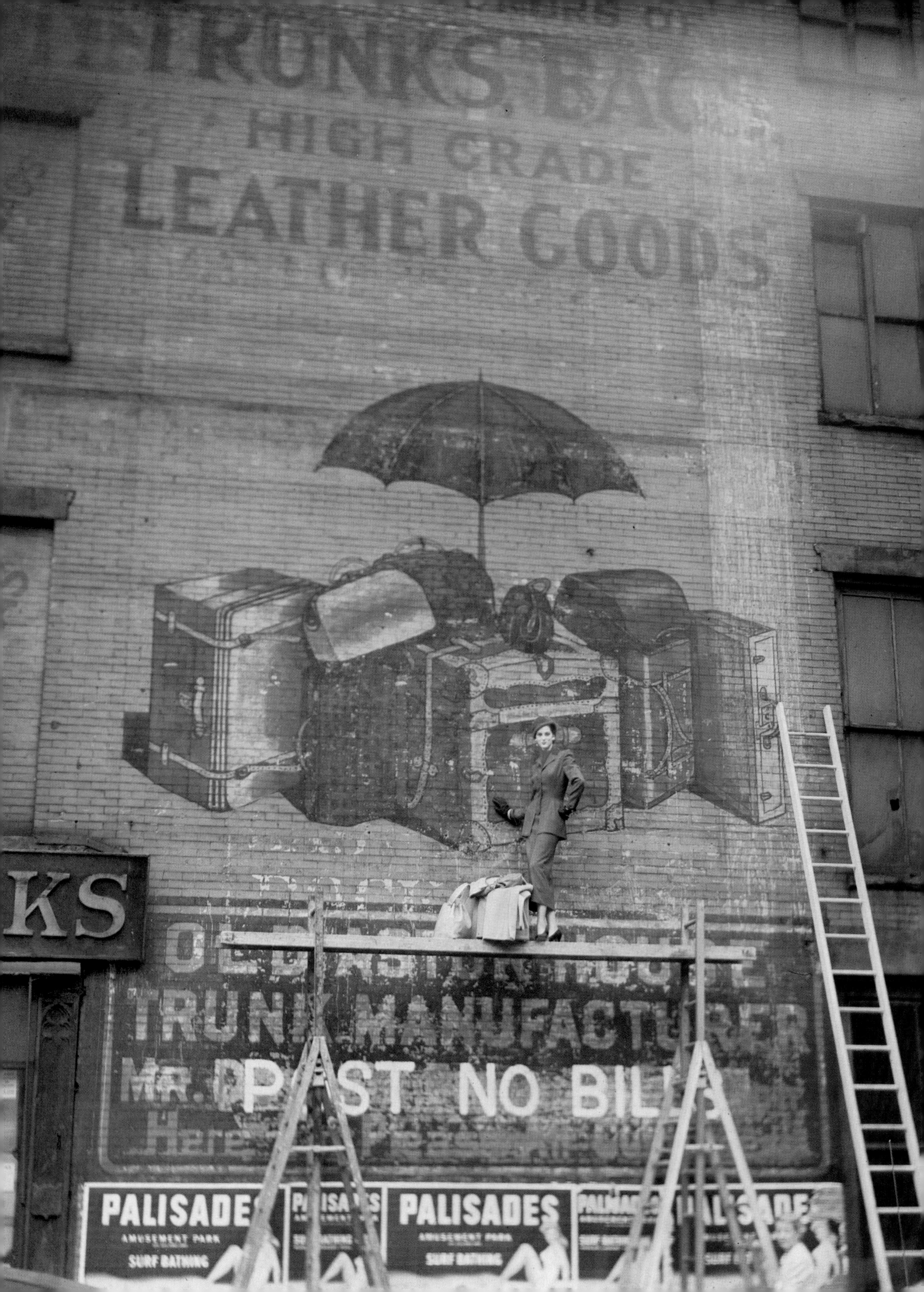

Books by Norman Mailer

The Naked and the Dead
Barbary Shore
The Deer Park
Advertisements for Myself
Deaths for the Ladies (and Other Disasters)
The Presidential Papers
An American Dream
Cannibals and Christians
Why Are We in Viet Nam?
The Deer Park—a Play
The Armies of the Night
Miami and the Siege of Chicago
Of a Fire on the Moon
The Prisoner of Sex
Maidstone
Existential Errands
Marilyn
The Faith of Graffiti
The Fight
Genius and Lust
The Executioner's Song
Of Women and Their Elegance

OF WOMEN AND THEIR ELEGANCE

by Norman Mailer   *Photographs by Milton H. Greene*

Simon and Schuster, New York

This book, while based on episodes in Marilyn Monroe's life, and on the reminiscences of Amy and Milton Greene, does not pretend to offer factual representations and in no way wishes to suggest that these are the actual thoughts of Miss Monroe or of anyone else who appears in these pages.

Text copyright © 1980 by Norman Mailer
Photographs copyright © 1980 by Milton H. Greene
All rights reserved
including the right of reproduction
in whole or in part in any form
Published by Simon and Schuster
A Division of Gulf & Western Corporation
Simon & Schuster Building
Rockefeller Center
1230 Avenue of the Americas
New York, New York 10020
SIMON AND SCHUSTER and colophon are trademarks of Simon & Schuster
Designed by Martin S. Moskof
Color separations and duotones by Offset Separations Corp., New York
Manufactured in the United States of America
Printed by and bound by Kingsport Press
10 9 8 7 6 5 4 3 2 1

Library of Congress Cataloging in Publication Data

Mailer, Norman.
Of women and their elegance.

1. Monroe, Marilyn, 1926–1962—Fiction.   2.   Greene,
Milton H.—Fiction.   I.   Greene, Milton H.   II.   Title.
PZ3.M28150f   [PS3525.A4152]   813'.52   80-15138
ISBN 0-671-24020-X

The author and the photographer are grateful for permission to
reprint the Interview by Richard Meryman with Marilyn Monroe,
Life, © 1962 Time Inc. Reprinted with permission.

The author and photographer are grateful for permission to
reprint material from the *Person to Person* broadcast with
Edward R. Murrow which included the appearance of Mr. & Mrs.
Milton Greene and Marilyn Monroe, © 1978 CBS Inc.

From an interview with Marilyn Monroe in *Life* magazine, August 3, 1962.

Goethe said, "Talent is developed in privacy," you know? And it's really true. It's having certain kinds of secrets for yourself that you'll let the whole world in on only for a moment when you're acting.

. . . Sometimes wearing a scarf and a polo coat and no makeup and with a certain attitude of walking, I go shopping or just looking at people living, but then you know, there'll be a few teenagers who are kind of sharp and they'll say, "Hey, just a minute— you know who I think that is?" And then they'll be tailing me. And I don't mind—they can't wait to call their friends. And old people come up and say, "Wait till I tell my wife." You've changed their whole day.

In the morning, garbage men that go by 57th Street when I come out the door say, "Marilyn, hi! How do you feel this morning?" To me, it's an honor and I love them for it. The working- men—I'll go by and they'll whistle. At first they whistle because they think, Oh, it's a girl, and she's got blond hair and she's not out of shape, and then they say, "Gosh, it's Marilyn Monroe!" And that has its—you know, those are the times it's nice, people knowing who you are and all of that, and feeling that you've meant something to them.

But when you're famous, you kind of run into human nature in a raw kind of way. It stirs up envy, fame does. People feel fame gives them some kind of privilege to walk up to you and say any- thing, and it won't hurt your feelings—like it's happening to your clothing. One time here I am looking for a home to buy and I stopped at this place. A man came out and was very pleasant, very cheerful, and said, "Oh, just a moment, I want my wife to meet you." Well, she came out and said, "Will you please get off the premises?" . . .

I remember when I got the part in Gentlemen Prefer Blondes, *Jane Russell—she was the brunette in it and I was the blonde—she got $200,000 for it and I got my $500 a week, but that to me was, you know, considerable. She, by the way, was quite wonderful to me. The only thing was I couldn't get a dressing room. I said, finally—I really got to this kind of level—I said, "Look, after all, I am the blonde and it is Gentlemen* Prefer Blondes." *Because still they always kept saying, "Remember, you're not a star." I said, "Well, whatever I am, I am the blonde." . . .*

It was a bedroom and living room in the Waldorf Towers on the thirty-seventh floor and I could look down Lexington Avenue to the East River. The view was real friendly, so it was a couple of days before I learned I was on the wrong side of the tracks, and the right people could see Park Avenue. I guess I'm not too bright.

By then, I wasn't going to ask for a change. Once I stay overnight in a place, my personality gets into everything. Moving out is as bad as pulling out. I grow roots like I've gone crazy. I might as well be a weed or some undistinguished flower.

All the same, I had the idea Milton was saving money on the rent, and that got me mad. Two days ago, after they brought the last of my bags in, he said, "Kiddo, you're in the right place now. At the Waldorf, you're going to learn a lot." Then he kissed me on the forehead and I kissed him on the mouth, and he went out looking worried.

It's good I remembered that expression. Milton can have a look like one of those sheep dogs who you think are ugly if you do not see that they are beautiful. They love you enough to die for you. So I didn't get what Milton calls truly angry. Still I decided he had been doing two things at once. On the one hand he was saying that I would yet become the best-dressed woman in New York, and in fact would have to be if I was serious in wanting to change everybody's idea of me, but then with that other face he tries to hide, I could see he was worried about money.

In that sense, he is two-faced, except it's normal to feel two things at once. You could almost say you're supposed to. Years ago, in Hollywood, I had an acting teacher who was commonly regarded as a nut. I only went to his classes for a little while, but he had an oiled mustache that ended in two short spikes (which certainly limited the roles he could play!—nothing but Hungarians!) and he happened to take me out once. There was nothing like sex rearing up between us, so, oh, the relief to go out for no more than a drink. All he wanted was to explain his secret philosophy to me. Superpsychology he called it.

"Do you believe in the soul?" he asked.

I told him that sometimes there was something going on inside me which felt like it was going to blow away, and he gave a jerk of his head and said, "We don't have a single soul, but two."

"Two?"

"Two complete personalities inside us. We are made from two people, aren't we?"

I remember we were drinking in the Beach-A-Tiki Bar out on Melrose Avenue, which they had decorated like a Tahiti slum —fake old dirty palm trees and lots of grenadine in the drinks. I must have looked like I belonged in the circus (which deep down I do) for I was holding a red drink next to my extra-blond hair—it was extra-blond that day—and I was wearing sky-blue slacks with an electric-green blouse that, come to think of it, was as dirty as the fake old palm trees. Not only a weed am I, but a natural slob.

"Two people. You mean, our father and our mother?" I asked.

"Precisely." The spikes on his mustache were sharp enough to spear shrimp. It put a lot behind his theory. Precisely.

"I don't have a father and a mother," I told him. "I'm an orphan."

It was stupid to say that as often as I did, but somehow I couldn't get through a week in those days without whispering it. My voice always failed me then. But those three words obtained more results than "I love you." Guys not only gave you free meals but put away their thoughts of mauling you.

This acting teacher, Abraham Robert Charles, however, hardly heard me. He was of another ilk. He was the worst acting teacher I ever had because he did all the acting in class. We couldn't open our mouth. You'd get up to do a student monologue and the first time you paused, he'd take over and do it himself. Since his studio was over a little farmer's market that handled cabbage, artichokes, cauliflower and brussels sprouts, the smell of those raw vegetables criticized everything we did.

"It doesn't matter if you're an orphan," he said. "You were conceived by two people." Then he bought me another drink. That meant I would have to hear all of his philosophy now. The funny thing is I never forgot it. His words went in so far I began to giggle the way you have to when something is screwy yet absolutely right. He was a Svengali, this man. My head felt like it was inside a magnet.

"Two souls meet when a baby is conceived," he told me. Afterward, for the rest of your life you had to contend, he explained, with those two different souls. Each became a separate person inside you. Both were receiving the same experience every day, but in different ways. It was like two naked actors in a closet who fought over each piece of clothing you handed in so one of them could get dressed for a role.

"They speak of day people and night people," he said, "only that's not it. If one of your two personalities is more oriented toward the night, the other, as I see it, leans toward the day."

In those years I was scared to open my mouth (I am still petrified, alas, with strangers). My thoughts would go on inside, but I wouldn't say a word, just snicker. This night, however, I felt I had nothing to lose. I had just broken up with my boyfriend. "It sounds like split personality to me," I said.

"Oh, no! Oh, no! That's a common fallacy. There's a split only if your two personalities don't communicate. Look," he said with a sad expression, like he hated to use this explanation every time. "Think of it as the Republicans and the Democrats. One party may be in office but the other still communicates with them. If they didn't, you'd soon have fascism."

Maybe I understood some of what he was saying. It wasn't like the sun went down and then the soul-of-the-night began to move around like Dracula. It was more like there were two complete people in you. In fact, he called his own two Abe and Bob (for Abraham and Robert). Both happened to live in Mr. Charles. That was the way he put it. Two separate people in every one of us, he said, and each was learning all the time, but learning different kinds of things. Together they made up the single person people saw.

"Take the male and female aspect," Mr. Charles said. "If it's a man we're talking about, maybe one of his souls finds it easier to understand masculine experience, whereas the other picks up more from experience we see as female. Say, for instance, that when I, Charley, see a woman putting on lipstick, maybe it's the Abe in me who thinks he'd like to kiss her, and it's Bob who can feel her putting it on her lips. Maybe Bob is a little bit of a closet faggot even though Abe is straight."

I was laughing and laughing. I saw through him now. It was Bob all the way. I didn't disagree with what he said, except it was goofy. There he was looking like some crazy Hungarian murderer. A bald head, a red face, a spiky mustache, but underneath he was living in a well-outfitted closet. "How," I asked, and I was giggling right in his face, "can Mr. Charles tell when he goes crazy?"

"If Abe won't speak to Bob, there has to be a breakdown sooner or later in Charley."

"Oh, you bet," I said, "it's got to go squeak."

"But so long as they can converse with each other," he said, "you have internal communication. That is equal to sanity."

Now, standing in the middle of my suite at the Waldorf Towers all these years later—six years later I figure it is—thinking of the expression on Milton's face and how he is worried about money, I also think, "Well, there is a rich man and a poor man in my friend Milton H. Greene," and it reminds me of Abraham Robert Charles's theory.

My living-room furniture is in pale-pink cloth and pale-green cloth and I have buff walls and gray walls. It is so French I could gargle, and the only thought to cheer me up is that Milton, whether the most generous man I've ever known or a closet tightwad, has still bought me four Norman Norells whose total price comes close to three thousand dollars, including one I know I am going to make famous for it is black chiffon see-through in the middle, and perfect for me. As Milton says, you can't go wrong with a Norell dress. It's like Chanel No. 5.

So I don't know why I think of Milton as stingy. Back in Connecticut, he bought me a white ermine coat. After I got done being thrilled, I cried for an hour. It was the single nicest thing anyone ever did, and the gift came after I said I'd like to play Jean Harlow some day if the right script came along. Milton croaked back in that hoarse voice of his I love except on those occasions when I can't bear it, "Ermine, Marilyn, that's what Harlow always wore," and the next day there was the coat. It made me look like I was sitting on a star. I can even forgive him for buying it wholesale. Anyway, I got out the vodka and tried not to look down Lexington Avenue. I always have to think I'm virtuous and I don't suppose a single day has gone by where I don't worry whether I'm a good person or not.

Milton was nice when I met him. Of course, many a new person was looking good to me after spending two months in Canada with Otto Preminger making *River of No Return.* I had also torn the ligaments in my leg on location, and Joe DiMaggio had flown up and rescued me temporarily from Mr. Preminger. It was just not the happiest time of my life. Joe D. wanted to get married, and going to get me in Canada brought it all closer. I didn't know if I wanted that.

Now, back in Hollywood, still doing *River of No Return* but on a set, at least, instead of shivering in the river, Rupert Allen of *Look* came over one morning and said the photographer Milton Greene from New York was going to be visiting. Something in Rupert Allen's voice told me to pay attention to Milton Greene. In those days I did not have the culture I wanted to have, and my mind wandered and I didn't read all the books I should. Yet sometimes I could learn the truth from people's voices. Somebody for instance only had to mention a name, Sir Laurence Olivier, and though I'd never seen a single one of his movies, I'd say immediately, "Oh, yes, I love Laurence Olivier. He is the world's greatest living actor." I can always tell by a voice when somebody is stellar. So, Rupert only had to utter "Milton Greene," and I saw an awful lot instantly—*Vogue, Harper's Bazaar, Town and Country, McCall's,* cover photos, biggest fashion photographer in New York, *Life, Look.* I knew they were saying: "Get your picture taken by Milton Greene, and you're famous. You're a legend." Of course, he would only like Garbo and Dietrich.

Therefore my heart stopped when Rupert told me to expect the visit. The ligaments in my bad leg began to scream inside the cast. I was prepared for the worst. Milton Greene was going to come to the set and look at me like I was the girl in the peasant dress who brings out the schooners of beer and wipes the sweat off her face. I hate feeling ungainly inside. High style always leaves me weak. I've noticed how fellows who never get in fights and read a lot of books love to be told, "Hey, you know, you'd really be a tough guy in a rumpus." They do anything for me after that. In the same way, a couple of men made me feel good because they had the sense to say, "Marilyn, you partake of elegance itself." Actually, in fact, only one man ever said anything remotely like that to me and I was mad about him for an entire month even though he had absolutely nothing else to offer.

Milton was not what I expected, however. A big grin was the first thing I saw, and then this young photographer behind it. He wasn't a lot bigger than me. He had the sweetest brown eyes and would have looked like a young John Garfield if John Garfield had been chewed over by a lion who didn't necessarily have all the teeth. Milton was homely in a very good-looking way. He could have been the Irish kid with black hair who lives on your street and fills your gas tank and has something dark and sexy to offer. "Why," I said to him, "you're just a boy."

"You're just a girl," he told me back, and oh, we hit it off, his two cameras clicked on his chest like castanets. Next day he took pictures of me. He brought along a big black knit sweater. That was all he was going to photograph me in, so I started to strip in front of him. "Wait a minute," he said, and turned his back. "I don't mind," I said, but Milton said, "I do." Later, in the shooting, he would cover me up whenever too much was showing. And he washed off a lot of my makeup and said it was cakey. Then we went to a little restaurant and had dinner. I just kept him talking. I wanted to hear everything he had to say about his childhood. I liked his voice. It was dopey and sweet. Milton made me laugh more than anybody I knew. When I told

him I was brought up in an orphanage, he said, "Yeah, well, I, myself, was found in the garbage can." But he couldn't go on with the story because in reality he was the baby of the family and got away with everything.

"What was your father like? And your family?" I had to know. I loved listening to people's childhoods.

"My father came from Russia and had an eye for clothes. A ladies' coat and suit designer. But me, I used to sell newspapers, shine shoes, hang out in the poolroom, keep warm, you know. Come the weekend, we had to look perfect, my father said, for visits to our relatives. When business was good, he would buy a diamond ring and bring it home."

I could see his father. A huge black mustache and a sex gleam in the eye. "If we didn't have money," said Milton, "he would hock the diamond ring. We moved nine times before I was eight years old. I was in wonderful gang wars."

"Would you fight in them?"

"Oh," said Milton, "I was anemic, but I hung in. I didn't live in fear. I maneuvered. Then we moved the ninth time, from Tiffany Street in the Bronx to Brighton Beach in Brooklyn, and I discovered I was interested in art. Some people are born more sensitive than other people and there's nothing you can do about it. I stuttered. Later, they wouldn't even let me in the army. I was 4-F. Couldn't talk. Doctor asked me a question. I couldn't get my name out. 'Forget him,' they said, 'he's nervous, we don't need him now.' "

Tears came into my eyes.

"See," he said, "you're sensitive too."

That's when I offered to drive him to the airport. As we said goodbye, I gave him a kiss, and pulled him back and gave him another kiss, and he said, "Wait a minute, now it's my turn," and gave me one. "I don't know if I really feel like leaving," he said. "I wish you wouldn't," I said.

"I'll be back," Milton said.

When I saw the pictures he took, I called him in New York. He was a great photographer and *Look* had put me on the cover.

 Abe might look at the girl putting on lipstick and Bob could be feeling it on her lips, but that was nothing to what I did with my twin personalities when it came to being photographed. If one of me sat there looking into the lens, the other personality really got into the head of the photographer. I always felt as if it was my eye telling his finger to click the shutter. I knew what he was photographing better than he did. Even when Twentieth thought nothing of me as an actress (and called me dumb things like "hip-slinger") and gave me no roles I liked, I was still the number one pinup at the studio so far as fan club requests for photographs were concerned.

Only, pinups have to exaggerate. A woman can have beautiful looks but that does her no good unless she's feeling beautiful. Otherwise she knows people are being nice to her because she has a good mask. Her personal question, however, is: When is the mask going to crack? I think there's a feeling of old age growing all over your insides when you force yourself to look beautiful. Now if you're a so-called sexpot, as I am known to be, you can only look beautiful if you look very sexy. So it becomes worse. It's uncomfortable to make yourself feel sexy if you're not feeling it. In fact, it gives me cramps. There I am trying to breathe into the lens, practically saying to the world, "Kiss me, I'm your garden of delight," but inside I feel like a balloon about to bust.

This accusation of being a "hip-slinger" hurt, therefore.

It's my private behind, after all, that they happened to be making the fun of. Of course, I can make fun of it too, but that's because I like slinging my hips. There are an awful lot of stuck-up people in the world who go crazy every time you do it. Up the Irish, I'd say, if I was Irish. All the same, I've always had to pay the price. I wouldn't say I look really cheap. I'm still too innocent in appearance. But that's the best you can say. I invariably appear—and I do hate this word—a little vulgar.

So when I saw Milton's pictures of myself in the black sweater, I was overjoyed. It's the word for what I felt. I wasn't just sexy, I was interesting. You wouldn't just want to run your hands over me, you might also be careful to listen to what I would say next. Milton made me look like I was stepping off a yacht instead of crawling out from behind the sofa.

In fact, it occurred to me that I, who always feel I know the inside of a camera the way other people are familiar with the inside of their stomach, didn't think about the lens once while the pictures were being taken. I was just looking at Milton smile.

 A month later Milton Greene came out to Los Angeles again. He was doing another cover for *Look* on Hollywood fathers. Bill Holden and his family, Bob Hope and Gene Kelly and their families. Since I was rehearsing the dances for *No Business Like Show Business*, we couldn't get together until Sunday on the back lot at Twentieth.

This time he photographed me like a gypsy, then like Bernadette in *The Song of Bernadette*. There wasn't really a single piece of cheesecake in anything he did. That disturbed me. The more clothes I wore, the more naked I felt. Being treated as a character actress was about as natural to me as driving a car on the left-hand side of the road.

Then it was back to singing lessons on Monday, and Milton went off photographing some more Hollywood fathers. It wasn't until the next weekend that we could shoot again. "How about Palm Springs?" Milton said. "We can work in the desert."

Well, when I was nineteen, I spent two weeks in the desert with a photographer and he kept wanting to take pictures of me naked. It was too early in my life, as far as I was concerned. Now I would have assented to Milton but he never asked me to take my clothes off, although he could have. He was to photography, as far as I was concerned, the way great actors are to acting.

We also talked a lot that weekend in Palm Springs. I wanted to know how Milton started on his career. Which was a sign I truly liked him and wanted him for a dear friend. I can always tell the warmth of my feeling of friendship by how much interest I have in somebody's personal work. There are times when I believe I love Joe DiMaggio and we even talk of getting married although I think it would be like going to the dentist—Joe D. has such fabulous teeth!—but I don't live with him as a friend. You couldn't pay me to talk about baseball. In fact, outside of Milton, I'm not sure how many friends I had in my life at this point. I had enemies and I had protectors. Joe DiMaggio, for one, was the greatest protector. I would have been comfortable shaking hands with a tiger if Joe was around. Of course, after the tiger left, where did Joe and I go from there? It wasn't that he was humorless, he was Italian. He only laughed when *he* turned on the tap. Whereas to me, laughter is like a wet floor. You can go sliding across. In fact, you have to take a chance on slipping. Joe thinks it isn't funny unless it comes through pipes the paisans sold you themself.

With Milton, however, I got deep into his career. I made him begin from the beginning. I knew in high school he went on the BMT from Brighton Beach in Brooklyn to the photographers he worked for on 47th Street off Sixth Avenue in Manhattan and didn't get to return home till 11 or 12 at night. "How did you do your homework?" I asked.

"Well," said Milton, "on the subway I used to say it three times, write it three times, then worry three times. But my head was over in photography. I had a boss, Marty Bauman, was a technical genius. So if you want to learn, you learn. He would go 'ugh.' I had to know which way 'ugh' went, left or right."

I just kept nodding. He couldn't tell me enough. All the while we were driving around Palm Springs, looking for desert rocks where he could set me down next to a cactus, we talked. Up to now, he had been such a good listener, which is to say he was so happy with everything I said, that I did all the talking. That is rare for me. I'm as shy as he is. When he was driving, however, he couldn't look at me as much, so it was easier to tell me about himself. I decided that in the old days, when he stuttered, it must have been simpler to talk in a car. If he couldn't finish the sentence, at least everyone could listen to the sound of the motor.

"After work, once," said Milton, "I painted a studio floor, 50 by 100, at night, so it'd be ready for a job. I got so tired I had to put my hand on my other hand to make the last stroke. The next day when I went to work, they had a girl in a bath all in soapsuds, and the client, the photographer, the 8-by-10 camera, and the lights. She's nude." Milton nodded like an old man thinking of a gorgeous naked young girl. "They say, 'Hey, Milton, make some suds. Put some over on the one bosom, down the shoulder, over the nipple.' *Nipple!* I almost started shaking. I used to stutter so much, it was terrible. If they said, 'Hold the fort,' forget it, who could I call to help hold it? They'd never get the message. So I was saying 'Wha . . . Wha . . . What?' and my boss said, 'Put the suds over the nipple, over the *bosoms*.' Marilyn, it was disturbing. I took the suds and said, 'Excuse me,' and I put it on lightly, and as I touched, it felt beautiful, but, you know, I'm the assistant photographer, that's all. Just put the suds on, I said to myself, make sure it's right, a little bit over here, bring it out a bit there. The girl's beginning to like the way I do it.

"We finish the job and go out to lunch, and the girl says, 'Thank you. I think you did a wonderful piece of work.' Maybe," said Milton, "that's when I learned that keeping quiet could also be good. I didn't want to stutter."

"I guess you had to figure everything out by yourself?"

He nodded. "I was brought up on a pump. A fifth of a second. You put the plate in, take a reading and go boom, boom with the pump. One fifth of a second. If you don't hold it one fifth, you spoil it. But you can stand to the side, and know when something's happening. You can see the picture come up to the lips, in the eyes, pump, pump, you got it. It's not selfish the way it is now, always looking into the viewfinder. What's in there? It's not seeing for yourself." He cleared his throat like he couldn't believe his luck for talking so long.

I really couldn't get him straight. Everybody knew his name. He was hot in Hollywood. I was always hearing Milton Greene this, Milton Greene that. A real ladies' man is what I kept being told. "Suzy Parker," I would hear, "Audrey Hepburn." I asked him if he knew the latter lady.

"She's a friend," he said cautiously.

I was angry. Audrey Hepburn was just the kind of girl he'd like. Too refined to take pictures. Whereas I practically had a red nose from sticking it into cameras. "For a fellow who likes to stutter," I said, "you're doing pretty good."

"Why don't we go to a party tonight?" he said. "I've been invited to a nice party."

 It was Clifton Webb's house, and I had never been to it before, but I had heard of the parties Mr. Webb gave. There was Van Johnson here on this night and John Huston and Barbara Stanwyck, and Gene Kelly and Nick Conte and Evelyn Keyes and Lana Turner and Joan Crawford and Judy Garland and Humphrey Bogart and Lauren Bacall and Robert Mitchum and Ava Gardner and Mr. Frank Sinatra. I couldn't open my mouth. People talked to me, and this little voice came out of me and answered them. "Hello, I'm Marilyn the mouse," I could just as well have said. I would have been sick except that they were all friendly to Milton and so nice to me. "Oh, you're Marilyn," they kept saying and told me how much they liked *Asphalt Jungle* and *All About Eve* and *Gentlemen Prefer Blondes* and *How to Marry a Millionaire*. They even liked *Niagara*. They were excited to meet me. "Miss Marilyn Monroe the mysterious," a little songwriter said to me (who was quite a hip-slinger himself). "Why you're just like Garbo," he said, "you keep to yourself," and with that, he slung himself over to the other side of the room.

I was extra nervous. Joan Crawford was there. I would have had her removed if they gave you a license to do it. When they honored me with the *Photoplay* Award just the year before, I had been wearing a one-piece gold lamé dress that the studio sewed me up in. The only way that gown would ever come off was the way it went on—in pieces. I knew that Joe D. would never take me to such an occasion—they could shoot him out of a cannon first—so I went with Sidney Skolsky, the columnist. By the time I came in it was late, and Jerry Lewis, who was the Master of Ceremonies, got down on his hands and knees and hopped around on the tables and screamed like a chimpanzee. I could hear one word from here to Singapore, "Brazen." I thought they were talking about Jerry Lewis. Then my shoulder strap broke. I could feel my boob go all exposed and it felt awful cuddly to me.

A couple of days later Joan Crawford said in the papers that it was "a burlesque show. Those of us in the industry just shuddered. Miss Monroe is making the mistake of believing her publicity. Somebody should make her see the light. Underneath it all, actresses are ladies."

I didn't go out of the house for two weeks. I called Louella Parsons and said, "I've always admired Miss Crawford for being such a wonderful mother—for taking four children and giving them a fine home. Who, better than I, know what it means to homeless little ones?" Of course, I knew from somebody at the studio that Joan Crawford whipped her kids black and blue. I believed it. An old boyfriend, a cop, once told me, "A judge will never forgive you for any crime he's capable of committing himself."

The studio came to my defense. "Miss Monroe does not have to wear tight dresses to be attractive," they told the papers. "She would look sexy in a potato sack." Publicity cut holes for my arms and my head and they took my picture in a potato sack. All the same, I could still throw up at the sight of Joan Crawford. Ergo, Milton kept feeding me champagne to get over the tension. Later that night Mr. Webb asked me to sing. I didn't even know whether I could get a note out, and there was Frank Sinatra and Judy Garland in the room, and Darryl Zanuck. But there was also Miss Crawford. So I gave the song, and it was good, I could tell. Later that night, Milton told me it was fantastic. So sexy. My voice would go high and then low, he said, but always sexy. Maybe it wasn't the greatest voice for phrasing, "but you have nothing to be ashamed of before anyone," he said. "Fabulous!" I knew then of two personalities who had been a lot of help. Milton Greene, for one, and champagne for the other. Let no one say champagne has no personality.

45

I guess when you get down to it, I really was a mystery in the town. I never hung out with Hollywood luminaries. A lot of people in the industry looked on me as a strange bird. They must have thought I went "Caw, caw" in the mirror. Outside of Joe D., and once in a while Mr. Sinatra, who was Joe D.'s friend, nobody ever saw me at parties or people's homes. I went to work in the morning and I went home at night. The first person ever really to take me out at my own level was Milton. Not just for publicity, but to meet my piers. "Hello, dock. I'm the dock three boats down from you."

So I told him about my love for Abraham Lincoln, which I hadn't told anyone else (but Arthur Miller, who held my big toe once for hours on a night we talked). The truth was that I was afraid everybody would laugh themselves to death at the thought of me having a crush on such a famous President. But I truly adored Abraham Lincoln. I used to have dreams that I was his illegitimate great-granddaughter. "Why not legitimate?" asked Milton. Before it was over, I let him talk me into taking a picture with my great-grandfather in my Cadillac car. I must have been in love with Milton right that minute to do something so revealing.

It's the fellows with the nice faces who drill that tiny little hole in your heart. Soon after Milton went back to New York, he called. "I'm getting married," he said. "Congratulate me."

"I heard all about it," I told him. "It's wonderful." I hadn't heard a word.

"We'll always be friends," said Milton.

"I hope so. Good photographers don't grow on bushes." Then I couldn't help saying, "They live like monkeys up in the trees."

"We'll always love each other," he told me.

The next time he was in town, I had to meet his bride. I kept thinking what he had said on the phone, "I'm going to have a family." That meant, of course, he wouldn't have a family with me. The worst blow I ever received was from an old boyfriend, Edward, whose mother liked me, and on top of it, I liked Edward. But he liked himself. The talk went over once to marriage, and Edward looked at me as if I was the monster on the screen who was knocking down the trees and said, "My God, if I ever died, my little girl—" he'd had one bad marriage already —"would have to be brought up by you." That went right through. Even now, if I think of it, the ripples start, the waves begin to roll, tears splash.

So I was prepared to dislike Milton Greene's wife, Amy, most intensely, especially when Milton insisted right after we met that the three of us go over together to Gene Kelly's house on Saturday night to play charades. One look at Amy was all you needed to know it was her game. She was as tiny as a nightingale, the smallest fashion model in New York, and she was as beautiful as if she'd just popped out of a cake on the society pages. Except her arms were so thin I didn't see how she could make love without getting crunched. However, I had to admit she was brighter than Audrey Hepburn could ever have dreamed of being. In the game, Gene Kelly turned out, it happened, to be the greatest charade player in the world, and Amy was the next greatest. Everybody was screaming. They were in heaven. I didn't even play. For me, it felt like stickball when they chose up sides. I didn't want to be picked last. I just sat there and did my best to look my very best, but in Gene Kelly's house if you don't open your mouth you're a starlet. One notch above a baby-sitter. Oh, that Amy Greene was organized. Not a hair out of place, yet she was having the most enjoyment. I couldn't believe it. I always felt the virtue of being disorganized

49

is that you were able to have more fun, but not in Mr. Kelly's house. I started to think of *Photoplay* and my gold lamé dress and those women saying, "Look at the bitch showing off her bazooms." That made me feel so miserable I started thinking hard about Joe DiMaggio. He, at least, really loved me. It wasn't too many nights later that I was able to phone Milton and Amy about my own wedding bells. "Mr. DiMaggio is not only the most attractive man in the world," Amy said, "but he is my hero from childhood, darling."

It was true. After our honeymoon was over, and it was not the world's worst, since Mr. D. had only to hear "Honeymoon!" to become a credit to the Italian people, we all got together in New York. Amy *was* thrilled. She told me she was a devotee of films and thought I was gorgeous in *Asphalt Jungle* and for a maverick young lady really held my own—Amy had this wonderful way of mixing show biz words I might understand with words like *maverick* that I half understood, and in fact liked better. But, she made it plain to me, she was "totally gaga" about my husband. Her mother and father divorced when she was six, and her father put her in a convent. She was an orphan like me, but a high-class one. Her father would take her out on Sunday to Yankee Stadium. All through dinner at the St. Regis, she and Joe D. were remembering some batting streak he had. I wouldn't say Joe had a look of ecstasy talking to Amy, but that was because his face didn't go in for such looks. He and Amy were sure happy though. I didn't know Joe D. could look intelligent when he spoke to a woman. I had seen his present expression before, but only when he was with the boys.

Since we were left to ourselves, Milton and I began to discuss my role in *The Seven Year Itch*, together with my troubles concerning Billy Wilder, the director. Those were enough to bring the tears to my eyes. Billy Wilder didn't say it, but I knew he thought I was a little inert on the set. That's because I like to start slow. Then I listened to Milton's opinion of various movies I'd been in and later he talked about my acting. I asked about my costumes and my makeup, and what he thought of the way I dressed in general, like right now. He said very gently, "Well, you know, you've never had anyone to say, 'You can't wear that, it's a terrible color.' "

"I need someone," I said.

"Go shopping with Amy," he remarked. "She knows a lot."

After a while I started to inform him of my troubles with 20th Century. In the last year my movies had grossed the studio more money than any other star on the lot, yet they still had me on salary. I was making pictures where I had no approval of the director, the script or the other actors. Stars of the first rank, which both the box office and *Time* magazine now agreed was where I was, never had to put up with such lack of stipulations. I went on and on, and he said, "Why don't you go out and make your own movies?" I said, "Why don't you produce them?" His face got scared, then it got very tough. He looked like the black-haired Irish kid who would fight by the railroad track. For a minute I was terrified he would stutter. But he said, "If you will show me your contract with Twentieth Century, I will see if there is a way you can break it."

Before we left that night, I asked Amy to take me shopping. I used an expression of hers. "I don't have a clue," I said, "what to put on." It had really come over me. Slacks and sweaters was all I ever wore unless the studio wanted me to appear somewhere for publicity. Then I would rush over to Wardrobe. Some of that stuff I borrowed for a night must have been worn by Clara Bow. Money may be cabbage, but cleavage is cleavage.

I went out shopping with Amy and wore a tight sweater that put an expression on her mouth like she was sucking a small rock—"the convent look" I came to call it—and I wore large sunglasses. She took me to Saks and Bonwit Teller's and people lined up to look at us as soon as I got spotted. Women were ripping open the curtain in the dressing room, which was enough to do Amy in, if she hadn't been made of the toughest stuff. First, she discovered I wear no panties, and to make it worse, a bit of my natural odor came off with the removal of the skirt. Nothing drives people crazier than a woman with an aroma that doesn't come out of a bottle. Maybe I should use deodorant, but I do like a little sniff of myself. It's a way of staying in touch. "Oh, God," the Abe in me can say to the Bob, "you're really rank today."

Anyway, Amy turned her head at the sight of my pubic hair which is, alas, disconcertingly dark, and then the curtains flew open, and shoppers gawked, three big mouths and three big noses, and a tall skinny salesman came over to shut the curtains and croaked "Miss Monroe!" and disappeared forever. I had to laugh. I knew I'd changed his life. I think, sometimes, that's why I do it.

After two days of such shopping, Amy said, "That's it, kiddo. From now on, we stay in the St. Regis and have everything brought up." I began to see how it worked. Some designers came by, friends of Amy's. I could tell by the way she said the name of one that it was another case of Laurence Olivier, Milton Greene, Joe DiMaggio, Arthur Miller or Elia Kazan. First in category. So I said, "Oh, yes, Norman Norell, greatest dress designer in the world." And he had a couple of the second-greatests with him—George Nardiello, John Moore. They were the nicest men. It was not only that they were well-groomed and

slim and fit into their clothes like a beautiful hand has gone into a beautiful glove, but they were so happy inside their suits. It was like the person within themselves also had a good suit which was their own skin. Moreover, they liked me. I could tell. I felt like getting into a bubble bath to show them that Milton wasn't the only one to have a way with suds. Oh, I felt open as a sponge. I knew they were going to help me. Norell said, "Marilyn, everyone has a problem. I have a friend who's very ugly and she's the princess of fashion in New York. She takes that ugliness and makes it dramatic." After she was done with her dress and coiffure she looked like a samurai warrior. You couldn't take your eyes off her. Besides, she was smart enough to wear jewelry that clanked and gonged with every move she made. You could have been in a Chinese temple. "Her little beauty tricks, if tried on anyone else, would be a disaster," Norman Norell said, and gave me my first lesson in style. "It's not enough to find the problem," he said, "and avoid it. Elegance is magic. The problem, *presto*, has to become the solution." As, for instance, he told me, the Countess Castiglione. She couldn't wear colors, so was always in black. She became so elegant she covered the walls of her living room with nothing but black silk and put nothing but black taffeta on her bed and all her furniture. Then she showed herself at home to a few male friends wearing nothing but a black transparent dress. No wonder Norell could design my chiffon see-through. He knew the story to go with it. I begged him to tell me more about the Countess Castiglione. I wanted to meet her, I said. Now, Norman Norell got embarrassed and explained with his left hand, so to speak, that the Countess Castiglione used to be the mistress of Napoleon the Third, oops, thought I. In fact, he said, she let her friends know that when she died she wanted to be buried in the lace-trimmed nightgown she had worn on the very night in 1857 when Napoleon the Third first said to her, "Come by the palace tonight." If I could have told stories I would have described to Norman Norell how John Barrymore met Craig Regal's mother, who was four feet eleven, but her son, Craig Regal, standing in the same room, was six foot six and weighed three hundred pounds. Mr. Barrymore, who'd had a little too much to drink, then said to Mrs. Regal, "Madame, what a *fuck* that must have been!" I wanted to say as much about Napoleon the Third and the Countess Castiglione on their first night. But I didn't. Nobody must ever know what kind of mind I have.

Anyway, Norman Norell got around to informing me very kindly that my neck was too short, only he didn't put it that way. My neck, I was told, wasn't that long. I wouldn't be happy in a *Vogue* collar. Definitely never in a Peter Pan. Ruffles were death. "Let me," he said, "show you a shawl collar."

I got it instantly. A nice thin dinner-jacket set of lapels and a long V-neck. Society cleavage. I felt as if I had spent my life until that point being sort of very fluffy à la Hollywood. Now I could see the way Amy saw me with my head sitting on my shoulders like an armchair in the middle of a saggy floor.

Of course, this new interest in clothes had all started on the trip to Palm Springs when I told Milton I wanted to be immensely respected and he told me, "First step. Don't act like a slob." He held up a finger. "Be a woman."

"You say, 'Don't look like a slob.' "

"That dress you're wearing," said Milton. "It's a *shmatte*."

"A what . . . ? No, don't tell me." I once saw a guy in a delicatessen spearing kosher pickles out of a barrel. That was what Yiddish sounded like to me. Shmatte. One more pickle on the prong.

"You want to be the greatest actress in the world," said

Milton, "but at present you're exhibiting neither class nor taste. They call you a dumb blonde, and they are getting away with it. You have to carry yourself different. Don't walk around like you're nothing. Never forget that you have something fantastic on the screen."

That was now prominent in my thoughts after meeting Norman Norell. I felt as if I was getting out from the carpet I had been living under all my life. I was beginning to see that class was not beyond me, nor was I beneath it.

Nevertheless, the next thing I happened to do certainly ruptured my marriage with Joe D. I wasn't wearing a shawl collar that night. It was the scene in *The Seven Year Itch* where I stand over a subway grating and my skirts blow up. Now I guess the studio had given me a white shmatte that night and tight white panties, and my hair had a hundred marcelled waves, and I certainly had no neck and lots of back and shoulders, where I was pleasingly plump to say the least, but I paid no attention. I threw caution to the winds, which is one cliché I could die saying and hold it in my arms, I can't help it, give me a ton of caution to throw to the winds. There were two thousand people on the street watching and they had a million whistles. All the while Joe D. was on the outskirts of the crowd dying because he knew the secret of acting. Maybe it was because he was a ballplayer, but he knew it didn't have to be false when you acted that you were in love, sometimes it was real, and when that happened, it could be more real than anything else. So I guess he knew—no secrets between husband and wife; that's what the ceremony is for—I guess he knew I was feeling a little moist every time my skirt blew up. Immorality would be immortalized if I ever took those white panties off. It's true, I wanted to throw myself to the crowd.

That went on for a while, and Joe D. took off. He went to

Toots Shor's. For guys like Joe, if your best buddy gets put in jail, or your family dies in a train accident, go to Toots Shor's. It's like a club where baldheaded guys come in out of the rain and put on toupees.

When I got back to the St. Regis, Joe and I had ourselves a rumpus. There is nothing more fearsome than to meet your protector when he is ready to attack you. Suddenly you know how your enemies feel. I have to admit I was awful tired of my new husband. Being with Joe D. was like living with a guy who builds you a house out of bricks. Every day you get to hold the bricks while he cements them in place. One by one. If he's a real Italian, he talks to the bricks, not you. "I want to go dancing, honey," you say. "We'll go dancing when the house is finished," he tells you. "Hey, even better," he says, "we'll have people over. They can dance here."

"Get out of my life," I shrieked at him, and he grabbed me in despair. I learned what the word despair meant. His hug squeezed my ribs practically past the place where they could pop out again. We sat down to talk, and he pounded his thigh. Then he grabbed my thigh for emphasis. Like it was a baseball bat. Those poor baseball bats. "Have a heart, DiMaggio," they say to themselves as he picks them up, "once I was a limb."

In the morning, after he left for the Coast, I got drunk on vodka. Vodka and tranquilizers. I did the dirtiest thing I ever did to Joe DiMaggio. I showed the bruises on my back and thighs to Amy. I didn't tell her that he never hit me, that the marks were not from violence but simple emotion, marks for his sincerity, you might say. I just gave her the idea he was a brute. I couldn't help it. I was mad at him, and annoyed how much she liked him. She worried about his ulcer and admired the way he didn't drink and didn't use four-letter words. He was so classy. He was the Yankee Clipper. Whereas I hated the way he re-

sented my profession. I just recently had found something inside that was the best feeling I'd ever had concerning myself. It allowed me to feel I could make beautiful movies and learn to live among flowers. The sad truth is just about all the men I had known up to now were the kind who put out cigarettes in flowerpots. So I just kept drinking my vodka.

Milton came up, whistled sadly at the bruises, and then he said, "What are you drinking vodka for? Here, I'll drink the vodka. You do the acting." It made me start thinking of the future Marilyn Monroe Productions and Milton Hawthorne Greene as my producer. That made me feel so good I even showed Amy a little makeup trick I knew. It was using dead clown white. You laid it on *over* instead of under the foundation, put it around your eyes and the laugh lines next to your nose. It took ten years off. Amy riproared with laughter. Hooted and pealed, she was so happy. I loved her for a minute. She was so smart that she loved you most when there was something you could teach her.

 Once I was back in Los Angeles, there were days when I talked to Milton and Amy every couple of hours on the phone. He had looked into my contract and now had a lawyer, Frank Delaney, who thought we could break it. I was beginning to see what the law was all about. Find a crack in the rock and use a crowbar.

Mr. Delaney came up with something. The studio wanted me to do *The Revolt of Mamie Stover* and that was about a prostitute in Honolulu in World War II. "Delaney says if you don't want to do it, then the role is degrading," Milton told me. "He says he can argue that 'every person has a basic right to stay decent.'" Delaney called. "Human beings cannot be compelled," he told me, "to do things that lower their dignity as human beings." I loved that. I could see Darryl Zanuck gnashing his teeth. "Who gave that strawhead the idea she's a human being?"

The trouble was everybody loved *The Seven Year Itch*. That almost turned my head. Charley Feldman, the producer, threw a big party for me that had Sam Goldwyn and Jack Warner and Darryl Zanuck and all the rest of the world at Romanoff's— Claudette Colbert, Gary Cooper, Clark Gable, Susan Hayward, Jimmy Stewart, everybody. Zanuck was even polite, and Joe D. was around again and we were having dates. In fact, I was having dates with people like Mel Tormé and Marlon Brando. Milton, at the other end of the telephone in New York, was very far away.

He came out to the Coast in December, three months since I last saw him in New York, and he had an answer to every question. What would I live on? I asked him. He would support me, he said, until I made a film, in better style than I lived now.

What if the studio never let me off the contract? What if I couldn't make any films at all? Well, it would cost the studio more than it would cost him, he said. I made so much money for Twentieth that they couldn't hold out. Their stockholders would go crazy. To hold onto part of what they had, they would let me have some for myself.

"No, Milton, tell me," I said, "what if you lost your nerve?"

"Nerve, what's that?" asked Milton. "I never found out what it was, so I don't have it to lose."

I told him that I thought Twentieth was ready to make good pictures with me now. Could he really claim he could make better ones?

"Oh," said Milton, "let me make one with you, two with you, and then I can prove how important you are. In my belief, there's only one man you should ever make a movie with. Cause you and he were born out of the same place. Ultimately, you live in the same high region. Don't ask me where, but it's the truth."

"Who should I make a movie with?" I asked.

"Charlie Chaplin," said Milton.

I decided to put in my fortune with Mr. Greene. A few nights later I packed some stuff, left my apartment, and we got on a plane to New York. I wore a black wig, dark glasses, and traveled in the name of Zelda Zonk. Amy was at the airport to meet us, and off we drove to Weston, Connecticut, where they lived and where I was going to hide from the studio, the world and all the reporters until Milton broke the contract.

 "Ah, we are young," said Amy to me once, "perilously young, and thank God we don't know any better." That was the only time she ever sounded worried about what might be happening to her household. Most of the time we laughed. The studio started calling to see if I was at the Greenes', but they weren't too serious about asking. They were calling everywhere. The Greenes happened to be one of twenty names on the list. Call these people every day, somebody got told. Maybe one of them will hear where Marilyn is. Amy loved it. Always tell a good lie if it's in a good cause.

"Is Milton Greene there?" they would ask on the phone. "No," she'd say, "who's calling?" "Well, where can he be reached?" the voice would ask, "we're looking for Miss Monroe." "Oh, I'll pass the word to him," Amy would say. After a while they started putting some impressive people on. Frank Sinatra and Billy Wilder happened to be two of them. Then Bob Hope called. He wanted me for his Christmas show in Korea. I had to laugh. The studio had asked Bob Hope to call. "No, Mr. Hope," said Amy, "we don't have a clue. Tell me, is Miss Monroe lost?" After he hung up, we rolled on the carpet and hugged each other we were laughing so hard.

I had a nifty room, a hideout. Milton and Amy fixed up his studio for me. The bedroom was on a balcony and the studio was like a two-story living room with glass. I could go out by myself, and take their dogs and walk in the woods, and come in by myself. It felt like the first real rest I ever had in my life. There was all that birchwood outside. I loved silver trees and kept wondering what they had to say to the others. "Excuse me for being so light, but I have to live too," was probably what you'd hear.

A lot of the time I was in the bathtub. Amy knew oils and bath salts, and I would take bubble baths. Sometimes I would take one in the morning and another at night. It would be a very long bath in the morning and I would rest in the water until Hollywood went right out of my pores and then I would put a lot of cream on my face—I figured it took a ton of cream to forestall one wrinkle, and I loved Germaine Monteil at $20 a pot. It made my skin feel good enough to be kissed by a king. In fact I would kiss my arms in the tub.

About one o'clock I'd be ready and we would drive into Westport and go antiquing. I also got impressed with all the potted flowers and bushes and trees they had to sell in town, and how Amy knew to plant them in the garden. I don't know how early she got up, but the house was always ready by the time I showed my face and the groceries had been bought and Milton was long gone to New York. I needed sleep like I was rolling around in bales of cotton.

In the evening we'd go to a movie or watch television or I'd disguise myself and we'd drive to New York. When we got back I'd play the radio by myself late at night and feel like I was out there somewhere in the middle of America with all those people whistling for me in the long dark night. That was the most comfortable feeling I knew.

Sometimes before I went to sleep, I would go over what had happened in the day. It could have undesirable effects (in the extreme!). Many of the things that happened to me were real enough the first time. Seeing them again in my head made them twice as vivid. A guy with fat lips who I once kissed at a party came back to my mind like two patties of raw hamburger. My nervous system was in higher focus than my skin.

Once in a while, to put myself to sleep, I would think of Amy's underwear, which was not only immaculate but color-coordinated. If she was wearing a purple dress, why, she would also put on a purple bra and a purple girdle and a purple half-slip. "Why?" I asked her. "People can't see what you have on underneath."

"I like the feeling of being altogether in the color I wear." I got it. She did everything for the inner feeling. I was so impressed.

"Besides," said Amy, "if my husband comes wandering through while I'm getting dressed I want him to see something pretty. Why should I show Milton cotton underwear? With his eyes!"

Her lingerie cabinet was like a rainbow. All those colors arranged in a fan. When I thought about it, going to sleep, the lingerie gave off sounds like organ pipes. I felt so much love for Amy because we could be friends, she who had every color of the rainbow for her underwear, and I who never wore any.

But, oh, those baths. I'm a chameleon. I even get to look the same color as the people I live with. I'm at their mercy if they have a poor complexion. Around Amy, I got prudish. I suppose you're an absolute great mimic if you have to become like the person you live with.

Amy could certainly criticize others. She was better at it than anybody I ever met. She might be prettier than any bird I ever saw, but boy, oh boy, she didn't have any more hesitation than the birds. Things better be right. Otherwise she'd peck your eyes out. Impersonal, like a bird. One day, for instance, she bought me a size 38 cashmere sweater from her friend Butzy Moffitt who ran the Separate Shop in Westport, and I got the idea. If I was going to wear sweaters, make them cashmere. But I started thinking it over and asked her the next day, "Could you bring me one in size 36, also one in 34?" I was thinking I would wear the 38 to make Amy and her friends happy, and keep the 36 for dinner parties, and then the 34 for national television.

"What?" said Amy. "Oh, *Christ*, take the 38." She said "Christ" like a firecracker. Falling asleep, I saw myself big as a balloon in the 34. "All right, darling," Amy said the next day, "you can have the smaller sweaters. They're your work clothes, aren't they?"

I nodded. "Amy, what don't you like about the outfit I have on?"

"Well, kiddo," said Amy, "the ass is too tight, the skirt is too short, and the color is wrong. Too primary."

"You're absolutely correct," I told her.

"You don't need it. You're a star. You can wear anything you want. Marilyn, you don't have to show your behind, you certainly don't have to show your tits. My dear, you're already there."

"But that's what they pay money to see." I wasn't going to let go of that. "Amy is a point of view," I would tell myself as I fell asleep.

In the daytime, however, I would be at her again. "How come," I would ask, "you always know how to pick the right thing? How come no matter what time of the day or night I see you, you always look right? Where do you get your shoes?" I would even ask her. I had the feeling that was the fastest way to learn about her.

"Do you mind my looking?" I would inquire when I poked into her closets.

"Having been raised in a convent with sixty girls, Miss Gorgeous, I do not mind," said Amy. "It's all part of the . . ." She didn't finish what she was going to say.

But I could picture being raised in a convent. Certain costumes for certain occasions of the day. "I guess you have to be in tune with the mood," I said.

She nodded. "We used to wear aprons at given hours," she said, "and if you were in art class, there was a smock you put on." She knew that without her I would end up throwing my clothes everywhere, so Amy said, "What we wore had to be well protected."

"I wish I could have lived in a convent," I told her. "My foster parents never taught me anything."

"Zhlubs," said Amy. "Just your average zhlubs."

 One morning while I was in the tub somebody phoned for me, and Amy knocked on the door. I told her to come in. I was feeling all pink and white and wet, and Amy said, "You're *very pretty*. You're really all peaches and cream." It was the only time I ever saw her flustered. She even said, "I'm shocked. You've been living here all this time, and you're really, truly, *exquisitely* beautiful," and then she turned and went out the door and said, "I'll tell them you'll call back," and I lay there in the water and thanked God I was beautiful enough to make Amy notice it. But,

oh, I would have liked to see the same expression on her face when I was dressed.

I must have given Milton the same idea because in Amy's presence he decided to buy me a white ermine coat. He had been studying the problem of my costumes for a long time, he said, and had come to the conclusion that everything I wore from now on must be in white. He said Norman Norell and John Moore and George Nardiello were all going to start thinking in white for me. I knew his mind by now, and Milton was thinking ahead. Chaplin was always dressed in black, so the picture we would make together could be filmed in color, yet seem black and white—to be stunning, you have to be simple.

Part of my wardrobe would be a fur coat, but when I said white fox would be nice, he snorted. For a friendly guy, Milton could put a lot of disdain into his nose. "A typical starlet," said Milton, "is given a fox boa at the door of Wardrobe. 'Go out,' they say, and they shove you in front of fifty photographers. I am not talking about white fox, but ermine."

I didn't even know what ermine was. I had heard of fox and mink. But Milton thought so little of them he had a black topcoat where he had them put the mink on the inside. That was being pretty free with your money considering Milton earned all his own money, job by job, but then he had a couple of hundred suits as well. That impressed me almost as much as his wife's underwear.

Now Amy joined in. "Mink is for *futbol*," she said in a Russian accent just to be funny. "If you want fur, buy ermine or sable."

I couldn't get over the way Amy was not upset when Milton bought me the coat. Of course, she had furs of her own, but this was his money. I might pay it back someday, but even so, I might not. Who knew? I didn't understand. I kept thinking,

What would I have said to Joe D. if he told me he was buying one of my girlfriends a nice outfit?

When the ermine arrived, I never took it off. I would go to bed with the coat on top of my bed. I loved every animal that had gone into it, and I used to pray to them in heaven and see their eyes glowing, and wonder if they loved me. I never thought of the hunter. I thought that was fair. After all, I made movies and people would look at them when I was dead.

 Of course, there's a real power to fur. If a pretty girl puts on a pretty dress, then she's prettier, that's all. But when she puts on a fur coat, it's like she's got a man with her right out in public. It's a little awesome. Fur even makes me want to improve my mind. For instance, Amy loaned me a book on Napoleon and I read it and couldn't get too much from it. The man who'd written it was named Mr. Ludwig, and you're never going to get a lot out of a fellow named Ludwig. After all, Beethoven used up most of the name. Besides, Napoleon wasn't my idea of a romance for life. Unless a woman could command attention like Josephine, she would be lucky to have three conversations a year with him. I could always see Napoleon looking at his watch. Darryl Zanuck with a sword. "Excuse me, the armies are about to march."

So Josephine really impressed me. On Amy's shelf I found another book about her whose title I forget, but when everybody else was asleep I'd read about the lady in my studio bedroom with the white ermine on top of the blankets. My fingers would be in the fur even as I read.

There was, first of all, her costume. Josephine liked to wear a white Greek gown that would leave her breasts bare. What a style for me, I thought. Napoleon might have quit her on the spot if he had ever seen me dressed like that.

Then I learned that Josephine had a friend named Madame Recamier (which name I wasn't sure I knew how to pronounce). It seems there were three women who were always together, Josephine, Madame Recamier and Therese Tallien. Their three husbands were all running France together (until Napoleon won out over the others) and so for a while these women were called the Three Graces. I would look at their pictures and think what a movie it would make with Ava Gardner, Elizabeth Taylor and myself, except we'd all be distrustful of each other.

I soon became fascinated with Juliette Recamier. Even more than Josephine. Reading in bed, I learned that Juliette was famous for her fabulous breasts. She even kept a nude statue of herself in her house which was pretty accurate in its details. But when Juliette got a little older and her chest began to sag, she had her breasts knocked off the statue. I winced as I read that. Then I learned she died of cholera. The book said "it was the most evil disease of them all." To my horror, I could even see her on the bathroom seat. My own bowels, which are so sympathetic they're crazy, began to growl.

That ermine coat must have had ghosts. As long as it lay on my bed, I just couldn't stop thinking of former times before I was born. I started to see Negro musicians playing violins at fancy balls in Paris, and I read about Therese Tallien, who would go out riding with a blood-red horse and a blood-red carriage. It was as if it had all happened to me. I also kept seeing the sister-in-law of Josephine, a woman named Pauline Borghese. She had a habit of taking a bath in milk every day, and kept a little Negro boy to lift her in and out of the tub. I got excited at the thought of talking the milkman into bringing a couple of fifteen-gallon cans over some day. I could fill the bathtub and blindfold Amy to get her into it—of course, she would never let me undress her, I knew that—but somehow I'd get her into the tub, and then I'd appear wearing nothing but lots of lipstick. I'd be coated from head to toe in chocolate sauce. "Hello, I'm your little black boy," I'd tell her. "I'm here to get you out of the tub."

Then I'd tell her, "Amy, whether you know it or not, you're Josephine's sister-in-law Pauline."

I'd lie in bed, so helpless from my own laughing that I felt as if I had climbed to the top of a very high hill. The book on Josephine had me excited and I read more and more that night until a couple of things depressed me. I didn't for instance like to read that Josephine Bonaparte and Pauline Borghese didn't really get along. I liked Pauline, and Josephine started to do her in. At Napoleon's court, for instance, the women tried to put on dresses whose colors would be right for the homes they visited. Josephine might put on a blue brocade dress if she knew her hostess had a yellow brocade chair. At home, Josephine even had a room furnished in red silk damask. (Of course, I didn't know what damask was.) Once Pauline went to visit her sister-in-law and discovered that Josephine had redecorated the red room without telling her. It was now royal blue. There was Pauline in dark green. She was so offended that she cut her visit short. After that, they didn't talk for a while.

It put me in a bad mood. I usually can't make up my mind what to wear. It takes me hours to get out of my own house. Therefore I never get around to thinking what's in other people's houses. It's Greek to me whether I'm going to sit on a rose-red or royal-blue damask chair. Maybe I'm deficient that way.

Then, I had to read about Pauline's death. She told her friends that she wanted to pass away in her best court dress. That was the only way, she said, to meet His Majesty Death.

I tried to get myself to laugh. I would meet His Majesty naked, I told myself. But now the idea of dying became very real to me, and I shivered and hugged the ermine and thought of the worst time of my life. There was a day I never told anybody about when I got ready with a certain boy friend to kill a woman, really do her in so she would see His Majesty Death. That little episode returned to me now in the middle of the night and it was the same as ghosts coming back. I had to take a couple of Seconal to go to sleep, my first pills in a few weeks. Oh, the nightmares of my past. They hung outside the door like a smelly wolf I'd once seen walking back and forth. His cage smelled of rotten meat.

 I don't know anything about churches because the only one I belonged to was Christian Science, and they just had a meeting hall and a book, but even in the fancy Catholic churches that Joe DiMaggio took me to, it still came down to the same thing. Every church had their Bible. That was like a cellar where you could put away everything bad. For instance, if you could sense somebody's curse out in the air ready to get breathed up a nostril (which is why, I always thought, old people won't take a breath when they're afraid), then that was the time to open the Bible. If you pray right, I always thought, the curse can be handled by the book instead. You can turn the key on it.

Well, I didn't have a Bible. You couldn't just go out and pick one. You had to belong to a church if you wanted to use their book. So I got the idea—I think it was because I was often alone so late at night—that I ought to get my own book together. If I wrote down some of the things I'd discovered that day, or remembered a saying that went right through me, or even some

nice clue I picked up from my reading, maybe I would be getting together my own private book, and it would be proof against curses a little. I hoped that was true. I certainly believed that the most private part of yourself couldn't be attacked by a curse. It was only in the stupid places where you were like everybody else that an evil wish could get in and feed. The parts of yourself that were bored would welcome anything. Of course a lot of people who quote the Bible all the time are real boring people. They need a lot of protection against curses, and the Bible, after all, is bigger and has a bigger curse than anything that can come into it. Whereas any little diary I put together by myself wasn't going to be more than a fence. It might keep a few bad things away, that's all.

All the same I bought a nice leather-covered notebook the next day. Then I had to wait for something to write in it. Not one idea came along all night. The next morning I was ready to give up except I happened to stop in the hall, and right there was a small framed old print on the stairs that I liked. It reminded me of Amy except it had to be of a woman two hundred years ago.

Now Amy had put up framed pictures all over the place. Some were *New Yorker* cartoons she liked, but I decided she must know the cartoonist because these were the drawings themselves—not the magazine pages. There was also one artist named Daumier who she had a lot of—I guess you'd call it etchings—and wherever you stopped in Amy's house there was always something to look at. A little white onyx marble box, or some crystal she told me was called Baccarat, or a tiny wonderful photo by Milton in a tiny frame—Amy collected beautiful little things. One of them was this picture of a woman. "Who is that?" I asked. "Is that you?"

"My dear," said Amy, "thank you very much." She shook

her head. "No, no, that is not me at all. That is Emma, Lady Hamilton."

"Who is that?" I asked.

When she realized I hadn't even seen the movie with Vivien Leigh and Laurence Olivier, and so didn't know about Admiral Nelson and Emma, she told me the story. I was—to use one of Amy's words—enthralled. Because, on second look, I thought Emma also looked a little like me, a little bit anyway. When I heard that she became a lady by marrying Lord Hamilton, but in fact had started by being a barmaid who would see a few fellows after work, and thereby bring home some extra money, I was doubly impressed.

Then Amy showed me a book written about Lady Hamilton. There were a lot of her letters in it, and in the beginning Emma couldn't even write as good a letter as myself. Over the next ten years, however, she improved considerably. That managed to take me right out of the bad mood I woke up with. I began my notebook by copying into it a couple of Emma's letters. It was a way of showing myself how much a girl can learn. For instance, there were these two letters she had written ten years apart, both to a man named Charles Francis Greville, who was a son of the Earl of Warwick. I could see from the atmosphere of the first letter that Greville, who she called G., probably took care of Emma when she was just starting out. He must have been extra nice because, considering the ignorance of her style, she was certainly comfortable writing to him.

"What shall I dow?" the first letter began. "Good God, what shall I dow? I can't come to town for want of money. I have not a farthing to bless myself with, and I think my friends look cooly on me . . . O, G., that I was in your possession, what a happy girl I would have been! Girl indeed. What else am I but a girl in distress—in reall distress? . . . I am almos mad."

Then Lord Hamilton, who was an older man, came along. He *swooped*—as Amy might say—right down on her and made a real lady of Emma. After their marriage, they lived in Naples in the Kingdom of the Queen of Naples where Lord Hamilton was the English Ambassador. Ten years later, nobody except Charles Francis Greville would have had a clue to how she used to be in her letters. Now, it was: *"You cannot imagine how my mother is loved and respected by everyone. She has a beautiful apartment in our house and the Queen has been very friendly to her. And told her she may be very proud of her famous daughter. . . . I tell you this so that you may see that I am not unworthy to have once been your pupil. God bless you."*

And all this had happened before Lord Nelson even dropped anchor in Naples.

I began to wonder if I should read so much about past history. It was like champagne. It got me truly excited. Everything became a movie or a play. I could open my notebook and feel as if I was in the theater.

In fact, once I got the notebook really started, all sorts of things that people said began to seem just right for it. Norman Norell, as one example, used to come over sometimes to visit Milton and Amy on Sundays, and I always enjoyed that because we would sit in front of the big fireplace in the living room and talk about clothes. Norell would describe the wardrobes he did for Gertrude Lawrence and Ilka Chase. It wasn't the story so much as all the personal style he had. He wasn't any bigger than Milton, and he was very thin, and just a fellow born in Indiana who came to New York and worked for Hattie Carnegie, "the old witch" as he called her. But Norman Norell had that wonderful voice people get when they're very distinguished. They talk like they could own the world if they wanted to, but who wants to do all those unpleasant things you have to think of to protect your property? These kind of people talk about books as if they know the author better than his own family, but they do it in a nice way if they're like Norman Norell. He used to let me feel part of the team. It was like I was allowed to come in on the same signals he used. Wonderful things would pop out of his mouth and go right to my notebook.

Sometimes I wrote down words I had to ask Amy how to spell. Norman, for instance, mentioned one dinner he went to where there had been a separate glass for sherry, for white Bordeaux (which I spelled Bordello until I asked Amy, who gave a little shiver), another glass for the Burgundy, one for Château Yquem (which I remember reading on the bottle when Milton served it, so I had no trouble there) and then a goblet for champagne. With all those glasses you could, as Norman Norell said, get squalidly drunk, but who would blame you?

"Luxury is what it's all about," he said, "only, what godawful people you meet." I loved the way his voice went.

"To the true philosopher, there are no trivialities," I told him back, and giggled. It was a line I'd read just the night before and put into my book. Incidentally, I had decided to call it: "A Ledger on Elegant Persons and Etiquette by MM with Comments by Herself."

Sometimes I didn't have much to put in. Once it was just names I'd heard Norell mention about Old New York.

Van Cortland
Van Renssalaer (spelling?)
Peter Styvisant (spelling?)
Ward McAllister and the Four Hundred
Social Register
debutante balls gate crashing?

Under that I had another item.

Paphos and Lesbos—are they dikes?

81

Then I came across something beautiful in another one of Amy's books. "The bed is the temple of love." I couldn't have loved that more. I was reading about the Duke of Luxemburg, who was so old when he died that he couldn't even see to read his love letters, so he covered the bed with seventy of them, all unopened. *Hello, Monsieur, Your Majesty Death*, I wrote. *Now, there is elegance. If I was an old man, that's how I would want to die.*

Then I wrote:

Elegance is to show you're the best of your kind. It's knowing better than to contradict what you said yesterday. When something is awful, and elegant people can't stand it, they clear their throat like they're vomiting. "Ahrrghh," they go, "Awwwrful." They're not afraid to let you hear everything. That's because they don't go around knocking things over or slopping coffee in their cups and then saying, "Oh, how did I do that?" They say "My body is out of control today," or "God, my hand shakes like a thief."

Amy told me that Norman Norell always tells his models to go to the bathroom when they have on one of his new gowns. If the dress is so tight that they can't get to anything, then even if the dress looks elegant, it's not.

What does that make the gold lamé gown at the Photoplay *Award? The only place I could reach was my mouth.*

I heard Amy and Norman talking about me today. "Five-five," said Amy, "not more. She's not that tall. She has a very long back and a very long waist which is interesting."

"Yes, she really has a wonderful body," said Norell, "but she doesn't belong in this century."

"Totally Victorian," said Amy. "Fine bazooms, tiny waist, big at the hips."

"It's like putting a dress on a guitar," said Norell. "Yet, I

82

love her. She has her own chic. Oh," he sighed, "if only she had another inch on her neck."

That night when I went through the books on Amy's shelf, I kept copying out little paragraphs about women in the last century when they wore hoop skirts and had hourglass figures.

Do you feel the iron hoops? Do you feel the impregnable fortress? . . . Do you pretend that a dress that stands out so far from the actual figure . . . never rouses one's curiosity about nature's secrets? Do not let it be thought that those who tend the great witches' cauldron in Paris, whence these fashions come, are not aware of what they are brewing.

"That's an old gink writing," I told myself, and laughed. There was something to be said for old ginks. They had a way of putting it.

Whoever has not undressed a woman of the Eighteen-Nineties has missed one of the better refinements of lovemaking, from the first tiny pearl button on her rose point cuffs to the lacings of that inflexible bastion of honor, the corset.

I was beginning to realize something else I was lacking. I didn't have imagination. Not the way you needed it. Not *once* in my life until this minute had I ever wondered how a woman of those days got her clothes off when she liked a man. Now I could think of nothing but bustles and corsets. One of the books described how a wife used to visit her boyfriend between four and five in the afternoon. It seems all the women got into their coaches and rode around paying calls on other women and having tea and practicing their manners. In between calls, they'd shoehorn the boyfriend in. It wasn't so easy with those corsets.

Figure it out, chérie, how many times a day I am obliged to change. I get out of my negligee to take my bath, that's once. I take off my street suit for my fitting at the couturier's—two. I change my afternoon calling frock, which is three, for my dinner gown, number four, and every other night there's a late ball which makes a fifth change and my nightgown, an exhausting sixth. So I told my handsome friend, if you want me to undress a seventh time, I must have a maid to help me. And that's not all. I warn you that I don't know how to do up my own hair, so I must have a coiffeur, preferably from Lenthéric, to arrange it. At which the charming wretch assured me that he wouldn't dream of disarranging a single strand, to which I countered, wasn't that as much up to me as it was to him, and wasn't he taking for granted my immobility?

I got dizzy thinking of how much you might want to sling your hips once all those were off. To tell the truth, with all that reading, I was getting restless. Once in a while I would spend a night in New York away from Amy and Milton and something was definitely going on in New York with a particular tall distinguished gentleman I was seeing, but in general, I was restless. It wasn't just all that reading I did alone at night, it was also that up in Connecticut there was no man to get ready for in the evening. To keep reading about elegance when you're alone is like wearing an evening gown on the moon. I was really developing a lot of expectation about a new romance—wherever it would come from. My present romance, which could be really breathtaking, if it had a chance, was offering a lot of problems. He was married and a family man. By definition I would say that is a man who can live in misery forever. He assumes that's the way it's supposed to be. It takes high explosive to move such fellows. They could be in a prison cell and look out the bars and see the sun shining and say, "Aren't we lucky? It's such a nice day outside."

"Here," you tell them, "here's a hacksaw. Take a whack at the bars."

"Well, I don't know," they tell you. "We can get in a lot of trouble here with a hacksaw."

Lately, therefore, I had been seeing the big man in my life with no big happiness. We had long walks on winter streets in Brooklyn, and sat over coffee looking into each other's eyes. I felt like I was jumping off an eighty-foot cliff into a teacup of water and he as much as told me that he felt the same. But there wasn't a lot more happening. An hour together in the coffee shop and he was ready for a week of misery at home. So I didn't know if I was at the beginning of real love where the sweetest part of me was going to come out from the most private part of me through all the loops and kinks which would be the first time ever in my life—once to a customer!—or, was nothing going to happen and would we just look into each other's eyes until the camera ran out of film? Everybody's life would stop for reloading.

So I was ready for something else, and it came on Sunday. I was made the offer that night to become a princess.

It was when Amy and Milton took me over to their friends' house in Weston, Gardner Cowles, whom they called Mike, and his wife, Fleur Cowles. They were the publisher and editor of *Look*. How fortunate can things get? I was always glad to see Mike Cowles for he had a beautiful red Irish face and shining white hair which made him look young.

On this night he had a man visiting him named George Schlee who was tall and very well groomed and suntanned and had his hair slicked back. He sat around in shiny Italian loafers and no socks. At a classy dinner party! I had to keep looking at his ankles. He wore a shirt that looked as soft as air. He would come into a conversation just long enough to say something very funny, then right out of it. Somebody was talking about Porfirio Rubirosa and all his girlfriends and the trouble they could get him in, and Schlee said, *"Embarras de richesse,"* and kept quiet again. (I had to get the spelling later, but what it meant, Amy said, could be translated as "Choose your candy, kiddo.") Anyway, when George Schlee said it, everybody laughed whether they knew French or not. His timing was that good. It's sexy when you can make people laugh cause you're there.

This George Schlee was as European as you could be. He was also Greta Garbo's friend, I heard. It's a great way to come into a room. "Hello—" you click your heels—"Schlee. Garbo's friend." Only you don't even have to say it. They're saying it for you. Schlee. Garbo's friend. He was, to my fond delight, gaga about myself. He kept looking me over as if he wanted to put in a bid. That got me interested enough to pull in my waist. I began to stretch my neck. He kept watching all night. Hardly talked. It was like being bathed in olive oil.

Mike Cowles sat next to me at dinner. "Have you ever," he asked, "heard of Aristotle Onassis?"

"Isn't he the man who buys yachts for Maria Callas?"

"Lends them, probably," said Cowles. "However, it could be said you don't come any richer than Aristotle Onassis."

"Well, they don't come any poorer than Marilyn Monroe."

Mike Cowles began to tell me more. "Onassis owns half of Monte Carlo," he said, "and it's not going well. They've got a prince there named Rainier whose family goes back a thousand years, but they need right now to spruce up the image for the old gambling joint."

He knew he had me waiting, so he poured wine for both of us. "Now George Schlee," he whispered, "is a glorified trouble-shooter for Onassis. And just a couple of days ago, Prince Rainier popped up in America. It seems he's inclined to meet a movie star and, if it takes, marry her. George is looking over the candidates for our little prince. I have a hunch he is debating whether you are the one.''

''Oh, I am,'' I said. I stopped. I had really been so bold I startled myself.

Cowles grinned. ''Marilyn, how do you know the prince will want to marry you?''

''Honey,'' I said, and I don't use the word too often, ''give me two days with him, and he will want to marry me.''

''My God,'' Amy said when we got home, ''you're going to be a princess.'' We began to play ring-around-a-rosy in the living room.

I started reading about Marie Antoinette. She had pale-gold hair, a real ash blond, and Monsieur the King—it tickled me the way they called the King "Monsieur"—sent a sample of her hair to a couple of big factories in Lyons so that they could make a silk called Pale Gold. Everybody in France wore it. You had to be *à la mode* with Monsieur.

I thought of Monte Carlo where everyone would be wearing Princess Marilyn's own Pale Gold. But then it occurred to me that Marie Antoinette's hair was her own color. With mine, you had to ask, "Who picked the bottle?" That spoiled my fun.

Marie Antoinette wasn't too interesting. She died young, and that never failed to upset me. I always felt weak when I heard of beautiful women passing away. Otherwise, she was just a rich girl and awful jealous. I read how while she was still a princess, and her husband's uncle, Louis XV, was living, his mistress, Du Barry, could keep a supper party waiting for hours while she dressed herself. In fact, Du Barry didn't mind if Louis XV's ministers visited her when she was still in bed. Sometimes she would even get up and walk around naked to give them a shock. I could sense circumstances where I might do the same. Let the people know what the King's got. Then they'll also know he's going to hold on to you for a while.

So I could see myself in a huge room just right for a princess high up on a rock in Monte Carlo. And as in Du Barry's palace, the servants would wear fawn-and-silver coats. There might also be six-foot Negroes in green and gold if I did it like Du Barry. She even had a black fellow to give her massages, and he would be dressed in sky-blue and hold a cane with a gold knob for show. She spent the King's money like a maniac. Each of her dresses cost thousands of dollars, but she ordered a new one every day.

Du Barry also knew how to annoy Marie Antoinette. For

example, Du Barry wouldn't put on a wig. So Marie Antoinette retaliated by having her own wigs put up higher and higher. Her mother, Maria Theresa, even wrote from Austria, "Your coiffure rises 36 inches from the roots of the hair and is decorated with feathers and ribbons! One should follow the fashions with restraint, never exaggerate them." Maria Theresa had a lot in common with Amy.

Still, Marie Antoinette was brave on the guillotine, whereas Du Barry cried all the way. "Oh," she said, "save my life and I will give the people everything I own."

"Everything you own?" the crowd yelled back. "You're only offering what belongs to us in the first place!"

I didn't know what my real feelings were on this. I liked the way Du Barry wasn't afraid to walk around with her hair in a mess in front of the King's ministers, but I was on the side of the people when it came to ten-thousand-dollar dresses. Or was I?

I guess the lady I had a soft spot for was Pompadour. She was Louis XV's first mistress, long before Du Barry, and she was very smart, and nothing could have stopped her except for two troubles she had. She got to look old fast, even faster than the King, and she hated sex. She preferred good conversation. Still, she tried to keep the King happy, and used to take a lot of aphrodisiacs. She would have vanilla chocolate for breakfast, and for lunch, soups with lots of spices and truffles. At dinner: oysters, crabs, artichokes, turtles, ragouts, more truffles. Then Louis XV would make love to her.

Thinking about that made me wonder what I would do if I didn't like Rainier. Would I end up reading philosophy and eating rich food, ha ha, now I knew what they meant by rich food. Would I worry all the while we made love, "Is this going to be an heir for the throne, or a lot of air?" The hideous thing I'd never told anyone is that whenever I didn't like sex and was feeling miserable because of a man squashing up and down on me, all I wanted was to let out some gas. "Forgive me, sir, for the foul stir, but I'm only a poor girl and what can I dow?"

Anyway, there was an awful lot of talk about Rainier for the next couple of days. Of course, we called him Reindeer, and Amy would laugh until her eyes were like stars. I even told her once how beautiful they looked. "My eyes are like stars?" she said. "Girl, you're absolutely out of your mind. It's your eyes that look that way." We were talking in her bedroom, and since she was holding a little mirror in her hand, she flashed it in my face. I couldn't believe what I saw. My eyes beamed. I have never looked happier in my life. I was truly charming. There was such a twinkle in me, I even felt it myself. I *was* nice. Maybe it was the first time I ever believed people could just like me.

But then I started thinking that this was a side of me people didn't know, and it was a pity. A lot of the public saw me as a scheming sex-bitch, à la *Niagara,* and *All About Eve,* and *Asphalt Jungle,* sort of a Lana Turner with an evil streak, and here I was in the mirror looking like a bride, or a kid in a high school graduation picture. It made me think, "It's a pity everybody can't see me on television looking like this," which was one of the few times I'd felt that way because the thought of being on television usually terrified me. It was the idea of fifty million people staring down your throat all at once. I supposed I would feel like I was six years old, and the doctor had his swab stick in my throat and was telling me to say "Ah." Television would probably be humiliating, like a hospital. "Intern, would you look at the nice goiter on our patient today?" I had the idea that when you died, you went to a waiting room and people sat around for a while looking gray. So it was scary to think of appearing on TV. Yet, sitting on Amy's bed, I told myself the public ought to know what they had here.

Of course, once my ambition is turned on, I always feel as if there's a water pump chugging away in the cellar, which in this case happens to be my stomach. Moreover, I have had to notice more than once how as soon as I start thinking about a subject, others do too. It's as if I draw them in. All of a sudden, Milton began to talk about the Edward R. Murrow TV show, *Person to Person*, and said maybe we ought to do that. This surprised me. Up to now Milton had kept saying, "TV is not for you, Marilyn. Wrong medium."

I knew he was interested in this Murrow show for a special reason. It was that Amy was madly in love with Mr. Murrow. In fact, the first time I heard the name was when Amy said, "Now, that Edward R. Murrow. There's an absolutely fascinating man."

I didn't even know who he was. That's how much I watched television. If other people put it on, I hardly looked. Joe D. used to sit by it for hours until I got to hate the back of his neck. What could be more offensive than a guy getting out of bed to turn on the tube? So I'd never heard of Murrow. I might as well admit I'd just about heard of Joe McCarthy. I was so ignorant concerning political matters that at first I thought they were talking of a relative of Kevin McCarthy, the actor. Therefore, to hide my innocence, I now said to Amy, "What do you see in Mr. Murrow?"

"A wonderful face," Amy replied, like a nun nodding at the name of a benefactor. "That man ought to be President."

A few days later, Milton said to me, "Hey, guess what? *Person to Person* wants to interview you, me and Amy." I didn't know if he'd been calling them, or they, by coincidence, were calling him, but it was an offer. Everybody wanted to know about me now that I had left Hollywood forever to throw in my lot with a young unknown producer. Of course, the truth was more complicated. Right now Milton's lawyers were working out a four-picture contract with Twentieth that would be interspersed with our own films for Marilyn Monroe Productions. In fact, I would be in and out of Hollywood for the next ten years, except nobody knew that yet. At present I was still the only movie star who went East. So they wanted me on TV.

And I, who always said no to requests to appear on interview shows, now said yes. It was the thought of seeing Amy's face when we told her, "You can finally meet your man, Edward R. Murrow."

After I agreed to do the show, however, I found out that we wouldn't even be in the same room with Mr. Murrow, let alone meet him. He was going to stay in a studio in New York and we'd be filmed in Connecticut. A crew was going to come out and turn the Greene house into a studio. That was the way Murrow did shows. He stayed in his quarters and called people all around the world. "Tick-tock. This is the spider. Are you out on that string?"

What I didn't know was how much work it was going to come to. On the air, the impression you got was that Murrow picked up the phone and the right people were there and ready to talk. Just happened to be some kind of TV camera around to watch. But for us, on the inside of the job, it was as if New York had declared war on Milton Greene's acres. A full week before the show a construction crew came out to build a tower on the hill at the other side of the lawn. "What's that for?" I asked. "An antenna," they told me. It was the only way to send a signal from Connecticut to New York. The tower, they said, was going to be 150 feet high, which was fifteen stories high. It made me dizzy. Heights always put me in the most peculiar mood. When I was younger, I would walk across a bridge and want to jump.

Not because I wanted to die but because it seemed a daring thing to do. Now, every time I passed the tower I wanted to start climbing the ladder which went up it. That is, one of my two personalities did. The other got so scared, I started shivering and feeling fever. It always ruined the walk for me. The snow was beginning to melt in the woods, and I had begun to notice the old wet leaves from the previous fall. They had such a smell. It wasn't really nice, but it told you a lot. Those old leaves were like a bed on which a husband and wife slept every night. "I've been next to the ground for months now," those leaves said. "I may know more about Mother Earth than I care to." It was such an intimate smell. I could feel what it was like to be buried. Not that awful. More like living in a wet churchyard. You might want a lot of long topics to think about.

So I could have enjoyed walking through the leaves, but the thought of being on TV made me think instead of freezing snow. I was getting scared. National TV. Every day they built that tower higher.

Then in the middle of all this preparation, I had to go to New York to ride a pink elephant. Mike Todd, who was going to film *Around the World in Eighty Days*, had asked Milton if I would ride this little elephant at the circus in Madison Square Garden for a charity benefit. I thought that would be fun, and Milton liked the idea, so we went into Brooks Costumes, where Milton got me dressed in a white blouse and black pompom skirt. He said I looked like a Day-God ballerina. That was what I thought he said, until later I realized he meant the painter Degas, who I had always pronounced to myself as De Gas. Well, for years I used to wonder why I kept coming across the name Michael in books but never met anybody whose name sounded anything like Mitch-aisle, whereas a common name like Mikel was never in any of the printed literature. It's confusing to have part of an education.

The elephant turned out to be a friend. He was young and they'd sprayed him pink. He knew he was looking special and he rubbed his head against my hand in a way that was half dumb and half awful smart. I realized he was cuddly like a year-old baby such as Josh Greene whom I adored—Josh could turn my heart inside-out—and here was this pink elephant who was the same way, not dumb at all—just speechless! All the while I was sitting up on the elephant and marching around the circle at Madison Square Garden, the crowd went wild and I felt true joy—say what they will, there is nothing like being the center of attention. So I loved that elephant while I was out there —and once we were behind the scenes again and the photographers were done, I realized that the nice good feeling that came off my big pink fellow was exactly the same as the nice good feeling that comes off a happy baby. "Hey," says its skin, "things are really all right."

But that night, after we were back in Connecticut (and my heart felt like a lead doughnut as soon as we passed the tower, which had gone up another two stories while we were gone), I had the misfortune to come down with my period. I say misfortune for I have periods that are like National Emergencies. If I was the first woman President I'd call in the Red Cross. I wish sometimes I'd feel something as incredibly fantastic on the good side as my cramps get when they're ugly. Then it's as if half the inside of my body is eating the other half. I get headaches like migraines and throw up. Sometimes I can't keep from shrieking.

Amy heard me. Even across the house on the other side of the remodeled barn that's now the living room she heard me, and came in before dawn.

"My God, this is incredible," she said. "I'm taking you to my gynecologist first thing in the morning."

"Maybe he can give me pills."

"Maybe he can."

"Don't you ever get cramps like this?" I cried out. I wanted to bang my head on the wall.

"Oh, no, who has time?" said Amy. I could see the look in her eye. It was nonsense to her. She'd swim or ride a horse. Having a period slowed the girl down about as much as stubbing her toe. Here I felt like I'd been left wounded on the battlefield.

In the morning the doctor gave me something to pacify the pain down to where I could feel like a caterpillar under a stone and not much more. Then Amy had a talk with me. "Kiddo, I'll tell you frankly," she said, "I asked him if it was psychosomatic, and he said no, you have a lot of scar tissue in there. He inquired how many abortions you'd had, and I told him I didn't know."

"I've had twelve," I said.

"Good God! You must be shreds inside."

"Tatters."

"What did you do, get pregnant every month?"

"Don't talk," I said, "or the pain'll start again."

She shook her head. "Don't you suppose these terrible periods might have something to do with your abortions?"

"Maybe," I said. "I haven't thought about it. I guess my curse has been getting worse each year." But I wasn't telling her the complete truth. I knew she was right. Years ago, every time I had an abortion I would go into one of those depressions you wonder if you are ever going to pull out of. And I would think of the baby I would have had, and how I would have spoiled that child. He'd have known his mother for sure.

By the day of the Murrow show, I was still getting over the pills and sedatives. If it hadn't been for the tower, I would have run away. But they had built the thing. It made me think of those guys who'd risked their life so the tower could send out a signal to New York of me smiling and talking.

Then the show turned out to be on Good Friday. They were asking me to speak to America on Good Friday. "What should I wear?" I asked Amy. "We're in the country," she said. "Wear your nice sweater with the collar." She meant the 38, but I decided on the 34. Just that morning I'd read a piece in a tenth-rate Hollywood gossip column: "The new crop of sweater girls, of whom Marilyn Monroe is the first oversold example to come to mind, couldn't hold a candle, oops, I mean a C-cup, to Lana Turner." Oops, thought I, that did it. My boobs were going to do the sparkling tonight, not my eyes. That's why they called it the boob tube, wasn't it?

Naturally, Amy decided to wear a blue oxford button-down shirt with the collar open and the sleeves rolled up. "It's what I would put on tonight anyway," she said. Of course, all she had to do was brush back her hair in a chignon and she looked ready for a formal dinner, no matter what she was wearing. Who cared, when you had features as tiny and perfect as hers?

Right at ten in the morning a huge truck pulled up with a lot of cameras and equipment and something like thirty men came trooping into the house bringing cables with them and lamps and cameras. I couldn't sleep. I went downstairs, and the living room looked like a swamp with black roots running across the floor. Kitty and Clyde, the couple Amy had working for her, were getting coffee out to everyone. I couldn't believe that Amy was planning to feed lunch to all. I decided she must have the same water pump working inside her as I did in me, only hers went into making the house work.

I could hardly understand why everybody was rushing around. We wouldn't go on until eight this evening. Here it was only 11:30 A.M. Then I found out that at twelve noon we had to assemble in the living room. They were going to pipe an image into NBC so Mr. Murrow could study how we looked.

On the spot, I heard his voice in my ear. It came out of a loudspeaker, but it might just as well have come through the ceiling, as though God was clearing His throat. "How are you all?" said the voice. I was ready to back out. "Please, sir, can I go to the john, sir?" Even Amy, with all her poise, was saying to the loudspeaker, "This is our living room, Ed." It felt more than peculiar. We didn't have a set to see him on, just heard his voice. All the while he was looking at us.

"Did my gift arrive?" asked Mr. Murrow.

We hadn't seen it. A couple of managers in the crew started yelling, "Was Mr. Murrow's gift delivered?" Kitty yelled back from the kitchen, "Something has sure arrived."

It was a great big gardenia bush about three feet by five feet. Amy was overcome. "Gardenias, I adore them, I adore them," she kept saying. Milton whispered, "She hates them."

Mr. Murrow sent me three dozen roses. To Milton he only said hello. I guess he figured he'd done enough for Milton already.

"Thank you, Mr. President, for the roses," I told Mr. Murrow, but he pretended he didn't hear me.

In the meantime, Milton was asking a lot of questions. "How does Marilyn look?" he kept asking. "Wonderful," answered Murrow, sounding far away.

"Ed," said Milton, "if you don't mind, I'd like to go out to the truck and look at the monitor." We were all on the same sound hookup, so as soon as Milton got out there I could hear him say, "Ed, I don't like how Marilyn looks. There's a spill on her nose."

"A *what?*" asked Mr. Murrow.

After a while, Milton got permission to rearrange the lights and fix me properly. Then he went through a lot of work getting the spill off my nose.

I had been planning to take it easy through the afternoon, but there was lunch for the crew, made by Kitty and Clyde: chopped chicken liver, tons of coffee, a big cooked ham and cheese—and the dogs to take care of, and Josh. Then, there was lots of tension for Milton. Murrow said over the loudspeaker, "Oh, by the way, Darryl Zanuck has been trying to get me. I wonder why." I knew what that meant. Milton was on the phone all afternoon with lawyers because Zanuck was threatening to sue CBS if they put me on the air. That kind of conversation ran through the day like red ants in a picnic basket.

By four o'clock, just before makeup, I was so nervous Milton said, "Let's go for a spin." He took me on the back of his little Italian motorcycle and after a couple of fast curves I stopped worrying about Darryl Zanuck with his teeth biting through a cigar, and I held onto Milton around the waist, remembering other motorcycle rides with other guys, and wondered if Amy knew how much I was in love with her husband right now, and thought she was a remarkable woman if she did, and I thought of something I read in her books: "You must hide your love for your husband better," some fellow named the Duc de Choiseul said, "for married love is one thing that will not be tolerated." Oo la la, it's Hollywood all over again, I thought, and shrugged because I was also in love with Mr. Sinatra—at least when I saw him—and still a little with Joe D., that could be, and with my old boyfriend Edward, whom I'd never told about my three abortions while with him since he did not think me fit to be the mother of his children. That was always dependable for a tear, even on a motorcycle. Then I thought of the man I was doubtless in love with, Mr. Arthur Miller from Brooklyn, versus the Prince of Monaco, and somehow I felt better. There is nothing like hot scalding emotion for relaxing your face.

I put on business makeup for the show. A lot of liquid foundation, then a cream foundation, then powder, and I took my own natural dark eyebrows and made them darker. With my hair up in curls I looked like one of the French noblewomen I had been reading about, some kind of angel who happened, incidentally, to be working as a kept woman. I even darkened the mole on the side of my mouth and thought of how in Pompadour's time women would cut out little pieces of velvet that had gum on the back and stick them to their skin. A do-it-yourself mole! They would put them in the corner of their eyes if they wanted to show they were ready for murder, or in the crease of the cheek to show they were good sports. Coquettes wore them near the lips. That was me. They used to use all kinds of shapes in those little cutouts. Hearts, moons, comets and stars. They would call them flies in milk. *Mouches au lait.* I remembered the spelling. Then, Amy came back from makeup. They had painted her into a caked-up freak. Must have used a trowel.

"How is it?" she asked.

"Awful."

I showed her a trick of my hard-earned trade. I took a cotton swab, dipped it in moisturizer, squeezed off the excess and then rubbed it slowly across her face, taking off the makeup in thin layers until she was where I thought she should be. "It gives a glowy look," I told her, "when you do it this way."

Now there was nothing to do but wait. It began to feel like an execution. Here I had been rushing all day to put myself into this hideous situation where fifty million judges were going to study me. And they all had suspicious characters. "Take her away—she's guilty." I kept thinking of all the fat women in small towns. Broad beams, narrow minds.

By the time we started, my hands were sweating. Milton

had an expression like chewing gum had stuck to the back of his throat and he would never get his vocal cords moving. My God, once a stutterer, you even have to worry years later about it sneaking up on you again. A true social disease. Amy was the only one who looked happy. I was afraid I was going to throw up, just a little bit, right on screen. "So that," the American public would say, "is what she is like inside."

Mr. Murrow had us ready to begin in the kitchen, which is where we spent most of our time talking. We sat at a 7-foot-long wood table Milton had built, and now I could see Ed Murrow on a monitor and he looked like a black-haired country club Irish fellow, real superior, and Milton was looking like shanty Irish with brains. All the lights were up. It was as hot as a movie studio. A little red bulb clicked on the TV camera, and Murrow started talking. "Milton Greene is a photographer," he said. "For years, millions of us have seen his pictures on the covers of *Look, Life, Vogue* and others. And inside, his pictures have illustrated advertisements. But few people outside magazine and advertising offices ever heard of Milton Greene until he became vice-president of Marilyn Monroe Productions, Incorporated. Milton, who is thirty-three, his wife and their year-old son live in this 150-year-old home in Weston, Connecticut. It's about an hour's drive from his studio in Manhattan. It used to be a barn and a stable. It's here, on 11 acres and 16 rooms, that Marilyn Monroe has been spending some of her time since she came to New York. Evening, Milton."

Mr. Greene couldn't get his mouth open. Stood there like it hadn't happened, and Murrow hadn't said anything to him. After a pause, Murrow said very clearly, *"Hello,* Milton." On the second try, the voice came out and he said hello. Murrow asked him how he was. Milton said, "Fine, thank you. And you?" "Tell me," said Murrow, "what part of the house are we in now?" "This is the studio," Milton said. "And where are Mrs. Greene and Marilyn?" asked Murrow. "They're in the kitchen right now," said Milton. "We can go in and meet them in a minute, I imagine," said Ed. "Yes," said Milton.

Amy and I sat like little girls in the kitchen while Milton tried to talk in the studio. Over the monitor, Murrow looked like the principal. "Milton, would you please take a giant step over here?" I thought he was going to say. "Yes, kind teacher," Milton looked about to reply, "I will take the giant step." Milton had his chin down on his chest the way a dumb kid does when he wants to take all the punishment on his forehead.

EDWARD MURROW:	I gather those pictures on the wall must be your work, aren't they?
MILTON GREENE:	Yes.
EDWARD MURROW:	Let's see. That one would be Janet Leigh and Tony Curtis, wouldn't it?
MILTON GREENE:	That's right.
EDWARD MURROW:	And the next one over is Grace Kelly?
MILTON GREENE:	Yes.
EDWARD MURROW:	And that's Janet Leigh alone?
MILTON GREENE:	That's right.
EDWARD MURROW:	And Ava Gardner.
MILTON GREENE:	Right.
EDWARD MURROW:	Debbie Reynolds and Eddie Fisher?
MILTON GREENE:	That's right.
EDWARD MURROW:	And Audrey Hepburn?
MILTON GREENE:	That's it.
EDWARD MURROW:	And those are all covers of yours, aren't they?
MILTON GREENE:	Yes.

EDWARD MURROW: Do you have any more pictures about, Milton?

MILTON GREENE: Yes, we have some over here. We have some pictures here of my son, Josh.

EDWARD MURROW: How old is he, Milton?

MILTON GREENE: Josh is one year. And then right above Josh is Jimmy Durante.

EDWARD MURROW: Ho ho. Wonderful. Ha ha ha ha.

MILTON GREENE: And then there's Dorothy and Dick Rodgers.

EDWARD MURROW: Yes. Now that's wonderful of them.

MILTON GREENE: Thank you. And then Marlene Dietrich.

EDWARD MURROW: Oh, I like that.

MILTON GREENE: And then this one. . . .

EDWARD MURROW: Oh, yes. That's Marilyn Monroe, isn't it?

MILTON GREENE: That's right.

EDWARD MURROW: Tell me, how many of your photographs of Marilyn have been on magazine covers, Milton?

MILTON GREENE: Only one.

EDWARD MURROW: Uh huh. And what does she think of it?

MILTON GREENE: Well, why don't we go inside and ask her?

I think the crew had learned how to do dolly shots in photography school just the other day. The camera heaved when it tried to follow Milton from the studio to the kitchen. But after they all arrived, it became my turn to worry if I would get my mouth open. Over the monitor, Mr. Murrow really looked like the President of the United States. "Marilyn," he inquired, "I was asking Milton what you thought of that *Look* cover he did?" "I liked it very much," I said, "although I like most of Milton's pictures." I couldn't stand my voice. It was tiny. I just hoped it was not a squeak. I wanted it to be demure. "Uh huh," said Murrow. "Well, now your picture has been on the cover of almost all popular magazines, hasn't it?" "No," I said, "not the *Ladies Home Journal.*" "That you would like, would you?" asked Murrow. "Yes," I said. "Why?" he asked. I realized I had to offer more, so I thought to use one of the words I learned from Amy. "Well," I told him, "I used to *long* for it. I used to appear, when I was modeling, on men's magazine covers such as—I don't know—*Squint, Peek, Take a Peep*—" I smiled sweetly. "All those stupid . . ." I let it go. "But not the *Ladies' Home Journal,*" said Ed. "No," I told him.

It was Amy's turn with Mr. Murrow. "Does Marilyn know her way around the kitchen?" he asked her. "Is she very much help around the house?" "Why, yes she is," said Amy, "she's sort of an ideal guest. No trouble to anyone. She picks up after herself. Just fine. You don't even know she's around." Amy gave a big laugh. On the monitor, she looked pretty good to me. "Does she make her own bed?" asked Ed. "Yes she does," said Amy, "and she helps me with the baby, to bathe him." "And cleans her own room?" said Murrow with a little smile. "Yes," said Amy, "she does."

EDWARD MURROW:	Milton, about this matter of Monroe Productions.
MILTON GREENE:	Yes.
EDWARD MURROW:	Have you and the president had any offers yet?
MILTON GREENE:	Oops, that's the telephone there. That's another offer. (*Laughs*) Yes, we've had quite a few, Ed.
EDWARD MURROW:	But you haven't decided on any one yet, is that it?

Milton Greene: No. We've got a few things in mind but nothing definite yet.

Mr. Murrow turned back to me. "Marilyn, tell me," he asked, "what's the basic reason for this corporation?"

"Primarily," I said, "to contribute to help making good pictures." There, I thought, that'll let them know I'm not as stupid as they think. "Uh huh," said Murrow. "What's the best part you ever had in a movie?"

I mentioned *The Asphalt Jungle* and *The Seven Year Itch*, and then he asked, "What's the smallest part you ever had?"

"Two I can think of," I told him. "One in a picture called *Ticket to Tomahawk*. I had one word. Well, not exactly a word. I said, 'Hmmm.' " I gave him my best smile. "And then, *Scudda-Hoo! Scudda-Hay!*"

"Was that all you had to say?"

Oh, he hadn't heard me. "No," I told him, "in a picture called *Scudda-Hoo! Scudda-Hay!*"—I tried to say it clearly but my lips felt thick, "I had one word to say. I said 'Hello,' but it went fast. In fact—" I smiled again—"they cut it out." Murrow nodded pleasantly like I was one of the brighter children among his mental defectives. Amy gave out a big laugh and that encouraged me. Maybe I had scored some points for our side.

"Who has helped you the most in your movie career, Marilyn?" he asked.

I had to give a long answer to take care of everybody who'd be truly offended if I didn't mention them. My God, I thought, it's like reciting a laundry list. Here I am boring fifty million people. But I had to go on.

Ed said, "I notice you mentioned two directors, Huston and Wilder. Marilyn, do you play a part in order to impress them? Or please them?"

"Definitely," I said. "I think with a very good director, of course you—in fact I think the story is very important. But even personally, more important to me than the story is the director. Because the director usually has a good story." I didn't know what I was saying. "Of course," I said, "the director usually has a good story. A director, I think, can contribute a lot." I came to a stop. I was afraid it was going to be my turn to stammer. "Because when you feel that when you're acting and the director is with you, and not just sitting by as the audience, that he's really with you, every moment, everything you do. I think that's very important. It has been to me." I gave another smile. My cheeks were burning.

"Marilyn," said Ed, "are you always recognized wherever you go, into nearby towns and New York?"

"No, not really," I said.

"Is that right, Milton?" he asked.

Milton phumphered. "Well, sometimes it seems that way." Amy saved us. "Oh," she said, "remember that day in the taxicab? When Marilyn came to do the window scenes in *Seven Year Itch?*"

Murrow gave a real encouraging look so Amy went on. "We were depositing her back at the hotel," she said. "There were about five million people outside. And the taxi driver turned around to the three of us, there was Marilyn in the middle, and he said, 'Hey, you know who's in the hotel? Marilyn Monroe!'"

Murrow laughed, "Ha ha," and said, "Thank you very much, Milton, Amy and Marilyn, for letting us come and visit you in your home in Connecticut this evening."

"Goodbye," we all said, "goodbye, goodbye," like we were waving farewell to the kind principal. Murrow turned to the fifty million people looking in and said, "In just a minute we'll be taking you for a visit with Sir Thomas and Lady Beecham."

The red light on our camera blinked off. We started to whoop and holler. What a relief! I felt so excited.

"You were wonderful," Amy and Milton told me.

"I wasn't stupid?"

"No, you were wonderful."

"So were you," I said.

The crew was all congratulating us and Milton broke out Dom Perignon for everybody, and Amy hugged the gardenia bush and had a photo taken, ha ha, by Milton.

The phone never stopped ringing. Milton and Amy's friends kept calling to tell us we were marvelous. I began to feel marvelous. There was a terrific kick in me now that the show was over. I felt like I'd leaped off a cliff and could do it again. I had been able to talk on TV with no prepared lines and no rehearsals, *impromptu!* I, who had always been the slowest in improvisation class because I was afraid of my ignorance when I opened my mouth. So we talked until 3 A.M. and I went to bed thinking that Amy would be up in three hours with Josh, and I loved her guts.

 The next week was the worst of my life. One of the worst. Disappointing things started happening right away. As soon as I woke up, I phoned a couple of acquaintances in Hollywood who I wouldn't call exactly my friends, but I believed they would be impressed by what I had done. Praise from dubious quarters is worth three times more than kind words from friends. Right away, however, the first girl, an old acting-school classmate whose career was in neutral right now, said, "Who is this friend of yours, this Amy? She's truly scintillating."

"Isn't she?"

"Real poise. Real vivacity."

After a moment, I asked, "Do you think I was a little down?"

"Well, kind of subdued."

"Was my voice small?"

"Marilyn, your voice will never be big."

Then I called another actor. He was a guy from whom I once bought a used car, and I trusted him because it drove pretty good. He was as Italian as Joe D. "Marilyn, who is this guy Greene and his wife?" he asked me first thing. "They sandbagged you, baby. It was a vehicle for Amy Greene, produced by her husband."

"Well, I thought Amy was good."

"Good?" he said. "Star material. You were the one who looked like the family friend. Watch out for those people."

When I hung up, I was perspiring up and down my back. I had hardly noticed what Amy was doing on the show. It had felt like I did all the talking. Amy had been full of pep, and sure of herself, but I was used to that. Maybe America wasn't.

I called two more people. They sure liked Amy. I saw a TV review in a New York paper. It said Amy stole the limelight. "Miss Monroe looked uncertain, nervous, and wan." The curse acted like it was going to come back five days after it had already delivered its curse.

Next came a call from Hollywood. To Amy. Jean Negulesco wanted to know if she'd be interested in the lead for *Bonjour Tristesse*. Since he had directed me in *How to Marry a Millionaire*, I couldn't help it, I said to her, "My God, I've been working all my life, and they think of you for a role, my own studio. My own director." Now Amy was the one who looked subdued.

I could see Zanuck saying, "Offer this Greene lady the lead. It'll drive Marilyn crazy. Set up a wedge between her and Milton."

But it wasn't that simple. They wouldn't give Amy an offer just to outmaneuver me. They had to make a picture, after all. Somebody big had to think Amy was perfect for the part.

Milton, however, said, "One career in the family is enough."

"If you don't mind," said Amy, "it's for me to choose."

"All right," said Milton, "it's for you to choose."

Amy thought about it. "All right," she said, "one career in the family is enough."

Later, I asked her why. "Well, I have my husband and child and I'm happy here. I don't want to lose it for all that deep dark stuff outside." All the same, she was pleased.

But I was dizzy. Milton got a kinescope of the show, and we studied it. I thought I was pretty good in personality, nice and sweet and shy, but my figure looked awful. I was overweight and in the tight sweater I looked like Miss Pointy Tits and had a rope of fat around my waist. Tacky. I kept smiling too much and petting the dog. I could have been a secretary in a small town. There was Amy looking like a Whiz Kid. "Not frightened of this a bit, folks." I had tried to be America's cousin, and lost to Amy who was Uncle Sam's niece. I couldn't trust her any more. "Everybody is out for Number One" has to be the saddest song ever sung and I hated to be singing it again. Now I remembered a story Amy told me about two women in Paris of the sort who are supported only by multimillionaires. One of them was called La Belle Otero and Amy was crazy about her. Maybe it was because she was also a Cuban. La Belle Otero had a feud with another such woman called Liane de Pougy, and one night Otero's spies told her that Liane de Pougy would be going to the opera all dressed in white and would wear all her jewels and sit in the largest theater box on the left of the stage. Otero immediately got ahold of the box on the right. In walked Liane de Pougy with all her diamonds, looking beautiful in white. She was wearing more jewelry than anybody had ever seen on anyone but a queen. The Paris crowd went wild. The people in the orchestra stood up and applauded and blew kisses on her.

Then Miss Otero came in. She had beautiful dark eyes, and was wearing a simple black dress and a black mantilla and no jewelry at all. Yet the crowd went insane. That was because her maid walked in behind, and it was the maid who was wearing the jewelry.

I laughed when I heard the story, but now, remembering it, I didn't trust the sound I heard in Amy's voice. She had been too happy laughing.

The same week I picked up the paper, and read that Prince Rainier was getting engaged to Grace Kelly.

I knew I had to get out of Connecticut and start to live in New York. Either I was truly, or not so truly, serious about Mr. Arthur Miller. So I told the Greenes I wanted to move into their hotel suite at the Blackstone. They said sure. They knew when one kind of honeymoon was over.

I packed and moved. But the Blackstone was a grimy place. "Ancient New York dirt" happened to be the way Amy put it.

Milton was unhappy. "It's not a proper hotel," he said. "Not for somebody of Marilyn's stature. Marilyn," he said, "belongs at the Waldorf Towers. I'm going to get her a suite."

Which he did. It took a while before I learned it was only a sublet from Leonora Corbett, who was going to England, and he got it at a low rent. No matter where I went, or how I landed, I always came down on the wrong side of the tracks. If Reindeer had chosen to make me Princess and started to remodel a wing of the palace in Monaco just for me, you know he would pick the servants' quarters. That is my Kismet. Whatever Kismet may mean.

Now, at the Waldorf, very quickly, I went back to my old sloppy habits. I guess I have no personality of my own. Maybe that is why I am an actress. I feel like I can be anybody else for a little while. Just as I kept myself very neat in Amy's house, took my bath twice a day like her, and picked my clothes off the floor, now I put on the kind of stuff I used to wear, the slacks that were not cut right. The sweater that looked like a stretched balloon. On his visits, I could see Milton getting unhappy that my pants didn't have a good line. To Milton, the right line was mint in your drink. The wrong line was bad as a sweat stain in your armpit.

I saw him looking around the living room and the bedroom. I could hear him thinking. "I couldn't live this way," he'd say to himself. "If you cleaned up after Marilyn, it'd be a mess five minutes later. It's the way she takes her clothes off." He shook his head. "Either hang it up or put it in the hamper, Marilyn," he was thinking. "Please don't throw it down."

I knew my makeup table made him miserable. I couldn't help it. Somehow my powder got over everything. He didn't understand. When I sat down at the mirror, I would see the commencement of little lines. In years to come they would be wrinkles, and that would make me pour a drop of foundation right on the glass table. I liked the feel of the oil on the glass under my fingers. Then I rubbed it in. Now, my thoughts would start. It was like an orchestra tuning up. Stories would begin to go through my head, that is, memories of things that had happened to me. As they did, they began happening again. I couldn't turn off such thoughts any better than you can switch off a projector if you don't know where to find the switch, I mean, you could stop it with your bare hand. So I guess I could have gotten up from the mirror, but I didn't. I kept looking at all the memories of my life including the dirty memories and the really filthy ones. Sometimes a tear would come out of my eye, and run mascara down my face like a knife opening a cut. Something very sad in me would begin to bleed.

There were times when I could stay for hours in front of the mirror, and one day at the Waldorf, maybe a week after I was there, I turned off the phone and stayed so long at the dressing table that when I looked up from the mirror, darkness was right with me. I must have been sitting there from morning to night. There was powder and grease all over the glass. Milton really expected too much if he thought I would bother to keep neat when there were maids around. Besides, cleanliness made me feel like my nose was being gripped by pliers. I wanted to cry. All those foster homes—"Be neat or you don't eat."

Right there at the mirror, sipping a vodka, I would think of Mr. Murrow saying, "Marilyn, you've been on the cover of so many magazines. Were there any you missed?"

"Well, I've never been on the cover of *Ladies' Home Journal*," I'd said, and we all laughed, but I knew why *Ladies' Home Journal* didn't want me. I ran my fingers around the circle the vodka glass made in the powder and the grease. Maybe I wanted to be a lady, but I couldn't even make *Ladies' Home Journal*.

I got so caught up with the mirror that once when Milton rang the bell, I let him in and then went right back to my dressing table, to study the places where my skin did not look young any more. Milton said, "What can happen in the next five years? Not a thing."

"Don't say that," I told him, "or it *will* happen." In my heart, I said to myself, "He'd rather have Garbo or Dietrich. He doesn't think I can act."

I was reaching for the vodka without even knowing it. Milton said, "Look, be smart. Don't drink so much. I'll drink for both of us. It's better. Because you're in front of the camera and I'm behind the camera."

I couldn't help it. I began to laugh. In spite of everything, I loved Milton. To the world he might be sitting on top of it all, but I knew he was like me, walking around with one wound while waiting for the next. The next was the one which would kill you. He had to feel as bad inside as I did.

But, oh, I didn't trust him any more. Now that I was at the Waldorf, I was getting ready to branch out a little. A lot of people I talked to these days were saying things against Milton. "It's his money I'm living on," I'd tell a few. "Not a cent," they would answer, "to what he's going to make from you." Arthur Miller said many a person would be eager to produce my films, which suggested he was not impressed with Mr. Greene.

I knew how to banish such depressing topics by looking in the mirror, but then my memories would begin. I would start to think of babies I never had, and those three in particular I

never had with Edward, whose mother liked me, and how something in the nature of that man had been so fine and delicate I used to feel that I was the man, not he, and couldn't keep my hands off him. Something in the very center of my body, that place where you could balance yourself if you could find it, used to yearn after Edward. One baby got started after another while I was going with him. I could even feel the big jump they took to come into me, I felt something go in, no one will ever convince me of the opposite. Then I would try to talk babies to Edward in the next couple of weeks, and he would get a face like a stone ashtray. "You're too strong for me," he would say, "you're too beautiful. You're too much in love with your career." All the while I knew that I embarrassed him in public. Of course, he had such sophisticated manners you couldn't fail to do the wrong thing. He needed a countess. He would, for example, call a waiter to order the wine and ask if I would like a nice red Burgundy. I knew no matter what I answered, I was in trouble, but I would try. "The wine we had last time was good, Edward."

"Well, that was fish," he told me. I was so stupid in those days I actually thought he meant they made wine out of fish, don't ask me how, I was just a girl from Odessa Avenue in Van Nuys after all. So I thought maybe there was a part that didn't smell like the rest of a dead fish from which they made the wine, and I was scared to ask anyone for days, until Abraham Robert Charles happened to tell me about grapes. While he was explaining, I kept thinking of things dying, for this had been the third time a baby took between Edward and me. Abraham Robert Charles kept talking about vintage, and I kept thinking of my appointment for an abortion next day. I was going all alone this time and paying for it with money from some modeling work—let us not go into that. Now, at the mirror, I just kept thinking of my two personalities, wondering which was the murderer in me. I knew I would have dreams tonight, and

nights to come, of the voices of babies who were gone. Where did they howl now? I did not like to open the windows at the Waldorf Towers (which were stuck tight anyway) for I was one of those people who could always understand that the wind was trying to tell you something. No breeze was ever that far away from me or my thoughts, and sometimes, listening, as I sat by the mirror, I began to remember people in my past who I'd known for a week in the way you think you are going to know somebody forever. So now I remembered something I had long forgotten, which is how on the night six years ago that Abraham Robert explained his theory of the two personalities to me in the Beach-A-Tiki Bar out on Melrose Avenue, I was listening with only one of my two personalities, and the other was thinking of Edward and the abortion and the funny look of pleasure I would see in the doctor's face tomorrow as he did it—for I had used this same guy before—and one of his two nostrils would widen out. Just one. Only half a sadist, you could say.

On that night six years ago with Abraham Robert Charles in the Beach-A-Tiki Bar, I did not want to leave and go home alone to think of the abortionist and how having to look at his face tomorrow would mean my love affair with Edward was really over, exit! Just that afternoon, Edward had told me, "If we got married, and I died, you'd be the one to raise my girl." There was a look of horror he tried to keep out of his expression. That said it all. About the time Mr. Charles began to explain about the two personalities, I realized I had been trying to interest a fellow whose double feeling for me could be described as Ed and Dead. So, I did not want to go home alone. I talked Abraham Robert into bar-hopping. He was the kind of man to have a lot of secrets, but after we'd gone to a few more places, I got a peek at

the rest of the evening. By now, we were traveling down that part of the Strip which is between Hollywood and Beverly Hills, and there was one sleazy bar after another, if by sleazy I mean that girls dance with girls and boys disappear into the bathroom with boys. After a while I could see that Abraham Robert was going to make one of his two souls happy tonight. That meant my ride home with him was lost and he wouldn't be buying me any more drinks. Pretty soon, however, a stout girl in a leather jacket and a crew cut was buying, and her name was Rosalie. She had a motorcycle. She belonged to the only women's motorcycle gang in L.A. and made her living as a gym teacher in a high school in the Valley. That meant I could probably borrow money from her. It was not that I thought first and foremost of such things, it was only that if you were going to bed with somebody you'd never see again, money at least left you with a little more respect for yourself. I knew a couple of things about sex with strangers in those days, and I expected she was going to squeeze my mouth and go in for a lot of her teeth knocking against my teeth in the kisses. Later, she might want one of us to sit on the other's head. Sex, to Rosalie, would be like getting the garbage out. Plus, she would cry when I left and maybe get physically unpleasant. That is, she would unless I went out of my way to be as nice to her as I used to be obligated to be nice to someone like old Joe Schenck, when he used to have me over at his mansion every night for dinner to show off to his friends. He would give me a second dinner later, just a schmatte, that is to say, his pickle, which was about how Mr. Schenck tasted. Although for an old man, and I'm ashamed to say I've known a few, you could get worse.

Rosalie was a possibility then, but not a very good one. Sitting next to me on the other side, ready to buy a drink, was a stunt man named Rod, and he had bleached blond hair that was long enough to reach his collar, and cowboy clothes, and he looked strong to me. In fact he looked like the kind of fellow who goes flying out of the car around the turn, hits a tree and knocks the tree down. All for a laugh. He had banged-up ears and scars around his mouth, and plastic surgery had left him with a little turned-up nose. A perfect job, ha ha. It was way too pinched, as if the doctor held onto his nostrils overtime while the skin was setting, or whatever they do.

It was clear that Rod could become famous in this bar. A number of boys passed by and hissed at me as if I was a black rooster. I wasn't used to being physically unpopular, just socially unacceptable, so I snuggled in to Rod, who explained that these boys were not a real serious part of his life, just profitable, whereas I, well, he thought I was the most adequate female he had seen tonight. Adequate, I realized, was his word. He was simple, I decided, yet awful good-looking, even if he didn't have his own teeth. They were, after all, well-made false teeth and helped his appearance. If you're just going to live with someone long enough for a cup of coffee in the morning, false teeth can be an asset. Even in those days, when I knew less about acting, I was on already to the secret Joe D. found out: If you're acting, it's better than if it's real. That is, it feels more real. False teeth can look better than your own teeth. Actors have to be that way. If you don't rise above yourself, you have nothing but yourself.

So I began to think more positively about Rod than Rosalie. He would probably try to borrow from me, but he might be fun. He would certainly be a ride home. Eventually. He, too, had a motorcycle. I always had the philosophy that fun was worth more than money.

Only I was afraid of him. He was too gentle. Too much time went by before he answered anything I said. He had a space in him where I guess anything could live. He might even be an animal who had said yessir to too many producers and was going to bite the lion trainer now. Then I began to feel something. I could see him climbing through my third-story window night after night.

Now, of course, even in those days I had a sheltered life. I wasn't respected, but I was sheltered. I might be considered the property of the studio and so be sent at a moment's notice with ten other girls to Denver or Modesto to help out with publicity, knowing full well that in such situations, the studio liked to hold the broadest view of publicity, that is—breed a little good will. I wasn't being sent out in my sweater to strew ill will. All the same, it was a sheltered life. I might have to go through certain experiences with a big laugh when I was actually feeling a little queasy inside, but, still, who ever had to be afraid of a local movie reviewer or a small-town theater manager? Most of them didn't have poison in their system. In fact, they were really grateful, and some of them were nice people. Anyway, back on the studio lot, I also had to keep appointments. One day I saw three executives on the half-hour, 2:30 P.M., 3:30 P.M., and 4:30 P.M. before going off to acting class in the evening, although, of course, those kind of assignments only took five minutes. "How are you, Mr. Farnsworth, how nice to see you again," and he had you behind the desk. Sometimes he never got out of his chair. Sometimes you never got off your knees. I knew the pleats on some executives' trousers better than their face. All the same, most of such people were not that rude, and I had an orphan's philosophy: Cheer up, it could be worse. They could take off their socks and ask you to kiss their feet.

The key thing, however, was that I was on contract at the studio. A girl might have to do one little despicable deed or another, but you were not out there where you really had to know how to protect yourself. You were sort of more in the very bottom reaches of the middle class, if that's a way of putting it. You had to be obedient, that's all.

Now there were times when I lived alone without even a girl for a roommate, and if it coincided with any time when I was unhappy, as with Edward, then I would have my share of desperate nights where in order not to be alone I would get into situations that did not have an ending like "Goodbye, Mr. Farnsworth, it was nice seeing you. Hello, Miss Paisley"—since the secretary would, of course, be coming in as you were going out. So I also knew what it was like when I was out in the night, and would have to stay out there, since the thought of going home and lying in bed waiting to go crazy because my head would not stop singing a sad song was, I could testify to it, a lot worse. I'd rather spend the night with unstable people and take my chances on getting home safe in the morning.

Such night life, however, did not represent my true feelings. To act like an alley cat was not nearly as comfortable as being a real pussycat. Still, there were nights when everything was wrong, when I had no dates, and my love affair with Edward was dying, and I was in no way above going right out on the town and being picked up, and some of those people reeked of trouble. Although never too badly. All my teeth were intact.

 After these memories started coming back to me, I soon began to think about Robert de Montesquiou who I had read about in a book Amy loaned me. I don't know why I thought of him—I don't even remember the title of the book—but he did dress like Amy did, or, that is, she dressed like him, since he lived earlier, maybe around 1900. He once put on a mauve suit with a mauve shirt and wore violets for a neckerchief. He was going

124

to a von Weber concert, whoever that was, and he said, "One should listen to von Weber in mauve." I couldn't imagine anything more elegant than that. "One should listen to von Weber in mauve."

Right there in bed in Connecticut I was trying to laugh hard but I really wanted to escape from reading any more about Robert de Montesquiou. He made me uncomfortable. Maybe it was because Montesquiou lived in Paris on the top floor of his father's house and you got to his apartment by going up a long dark spiral staircase and then down a hallway like a tunnel that was covered in carpet. When you got to his rooms, each one had its own color. One room, for instance, would be gray. Everything gray, the drapes, the carpet, the furniture, even the flowers, assuming he could find gray flowers. Then the next room would be red and have every color of red from shell-pink to carmine to blood-orange red—I learned more names for red than I knew there were. There was one party where Robert Montesquiou had perfume wafted around by a fan, and put perfume in the drinks, and had a perfumed turtle who was the only light in the room. He'd inlaid the turtle's shell with real sapphires and amethysts and rubies and diamonds. Before the evening was over, somebody even took the tip of one of their elegant shoes and tipped the turtle over, and a couple of hours later opium was being smoked, so the turtle died, there on its back, and I found it hard to breathe as I read the story, and started crying in my bed in Connecticut.

Now, sitting in front of the mirror in my bedroom at the Waldorf Towers thinking of Rosalie and Rod all those years ago, I also knew why it bothered me to read about Robert de Montesquiou. Now that I could see it, I had to see that it couldn't have been simpler. He made me think of the one man I never wanted to remember. It even came back to me that I met this man on the same night I took off with Rod on his big motorcycle. In fact, the name of the person I wished to forget was also Robert—Robert de Peralta O'Connor—and I had a week with him of a sort which was so bad that I never told anyone, not even Milton, who could have been my nearest and dearest when it came to telling things. I met the passion of my life that week, maybe I did, or maybe I was just trying to avoid thinking of the third baby I would never have with Edward, and so trying to burn Edward out—a hot night with someone strange is cauterizing, they say—but I stayed in bed with Robert, and called up 20th Century day after day to say I was ill with a lingering virus. I didn't have a bit part in a picture that week or my budding career that had almost no buds in those days would have been wiped out forever! That single phone call a day was all I could offer to my responsibilities, after which I went back to bed and stayed there with Bobby de Peralta O'Connor and we did things to each other which would embarrass me to tell, but I was in a mood that week to turn everything inside out. I hated Edward because he could not stand my lack of manners, whereas Bobby didn't care. Bobby de P. was an egomaniac, and in love with his own looks, a big plump red-faced rich boy with nice features and gold hair, as proud and handsome as you want—to me he looked like he'd been given vitamin tablets with gold dust. In fact, he loved himself so much I even caught him sniffing his own underarm. Tell the truth, I liked the odor he gave off, it was like he had been born to roll around. I had no protection against him.

I met Bobby, as I said, on the night I met Rod, and yet I could think of one and never have to recollect the other because Rod and I were through with each other before I even met Bobby de P. inasmuch as Rod the stunt man quickly showed me his favorite stunt on the ride from the bar down Sunset Boulevard across Beverly Hills into all the hills and steeplechase turns of

Bel Air. Rod's stunt was that he was able, with somebody as limber as myself, to make love on his motorcycle at eighty miles an hour, and I, riding in front of him, only had to lean up on the handlebars a little, and he was in the proper place, if from behind, my dear. I could have become an addict. It was as if the very fear with which I was born came out of me. I felt like I was landing an airplane with myself at the controls, and drums were beating, and lots of the rockets' red glare—I could have been in the electric chair. It was that electric. I was wild about Rod but absolutely impersonal. By the time we reached his friend's house in Bel Air, I was ready to salute. Yet he ruined it just as soon as he parked his bike. He grabbed me in the bushes and pushed me to my knees, that old Hollywood position, the industry is built on a lot of girls' knees, but I had no objection—after Edward the Delicate, Rod was a conqueror. It's just that something awful happened which is, I must speak intimately, he smelled like an oil well, or the way I think an oil well would smell which must be like oil and dirt and gasoline on a garage floor. I wanted to throw up at that. Come to think of it, he was from the oil fields, he said.

After we were done, it was like we were really done. I wanted to wash, and he knew it. As soon as we went through the door into the party, he was looking for another girl to be on his motorcycle—there's a love life for you—and I was looking for somebody who could remove the godawful taste he had left in my heart.

Therefore, I crossed Rod off the list just ten minutes after I put him on the list, and I was very impressed with Bobby de P., who came up to greet us at the end of the tunnel. The spookiest part of reading about Robert de Montesquiou all these years later, you see, was that Bobby de P.'s house was like Montesquiou's in that it also belonged to the father, and also had an apartment for Bobby on the top floor. Except in this case, you never went inside the mansion, but walked around to the back, and climbed an outdoor spiral staircase, and pressed a bell and went down a hallway that did actually have some kind of colored cloth on the walls, and very funny odors that I knew came from reefers. I had tried those things once or twice some months before, but never liked them because my head raced in circles afterward as though I was a tire spinning in the mud. My secret fear was that if I let everything go, if I just relaxed, I would be nothing but mud.

Anyway, I was still feeling stimulated from the ride, but sick from the thought of Rod—I can't explain—as if his insides were made of the rottenest dynamite, if dynamite can smell rotten, that is. We passed through several rooms, and one had knives and guns on the wall, and another with zebra stripes for wallpaper, and then a room like a photo gallery with nothing but filthy pictures all nicely framed, and the last room was big and had a phonograph and a table with drinks, and a lot of couches on which guys and girls, and guys and guys, were lying around in a very dim purple light, just enough to see that there was a lot of purple nakedness in this neck of the woods, worse —I couldn't believe it. This was the first Hollywood party of the sort I'd grown up hearing about. I was used to walking in on a roommate who was under the covers with a fellow, but never anything like this. There must have been twenty people.

Then I saw our host. Bobby was naked except for cowboy boots and a Stetson hat and he was walking a Doberman pinscher on a leash around the room, a huge female, I suppose, because she had a diamond collar around her neck. But as the dog came up to one couple, it tried to mount, and I saw my mistake. She had a lot of male in the rear. Bobby was giggling like a two-year-old because the dog kept jumping forcibly into all these lovers' midsts, if you can say such a thing. There were screams and shouts galore—"Bobby, get Romulus away! Bobby, you're a madman."

I would have thought our host was horrible, but when he came up to me, he gave the sweetest smile I'd seen in a year, as if he'd spent his childhood eating nothing but berries and grapes, and when he kissed me by way of greeting, his mouth was tender. I couldn't get over that, his mouth was as good as Edward's, who had the best mouth I'd ever kissed, but Bobby was also strong. I'd never been introduced to a man who was naked before, you learn so much that way, and his skin felt smooth as a seal and terrific to the touch. I couldn't keep my hands off. It was as if he was one boy who everybody had been rubbing love into since he was a baby. Oh, did his lower lip pout.

"Come on," he said, "you and me are going to leave these people."

He handed Romulus' leash to Rod and took me down the tunnel to a room at the other end that turned out to be another apartment. I didn't have time to look around, it didn't matter. We were on the floor. I was embarrassed for a little while, for I reeked of Rod, but Bobby de P. loved smells, I think he had a nose instead of a brain, and besides, he had his own aroma, as I have said. Maybe something in him had the answer to my secret, or maybe I had just been prepared for Bobby by that crazy ride with Rod, and so had kept nothing, absolutely nothing, with which to protect myself, but it was as if the very inside of me was pushing to get over to him as desperate as the feeling you know in a dream.

We went on all night. Somewhere in the middle I said, "Oh, you're the best. I never knew anything like this before," and I hadn't, I felt things start in me and go flying off into the

universe or somewhere, they were sensations going out to far space, so I meant what I said, except even as I opened my mouth, I knew I always had the same thing to say to any fellow who was any good at all, in fact I had said it to Rod as soon as he could hear me after the motorcycle stopped. I had even been tempted to compliment Mr. Farnsworth (after all, Farnsworth would say to himself, "Nobody sits in a chair like me!"), it was exactly the remark to make if you wanted to keep a fellow happy and on your string. I once had eight great lovers on eight strings. Three more and I would have run out of fingers. Saying it to Bobby was true, however, I meant it, maybe I meant it for the first time since I'd begun to say it, and Bobby just roared with a crazy kind of laughter as if he'd heard that song before. Then we just started reaching into one another as if we were really going to catch something never caught by anybody else.

After a while, we moved over to the bed, and later he even turned on the lights, and there were a lot of mirrors. The room was full of antiques who sat there like rich and famous people and I could see the Persian rug we had been doing it on, red and gold and purple and green. The bed was the largest I'd been in till then. We must have used every inch of it, he was one rich boy who wouldn't stop. All through the night there were knocks on the door, and people yelling "Bobby, where are you?" or "Join in the fun, for God's sake," but in the morning, when we wandered out (and by then I was so comfortable I wore nothing but high-heeled shoes, and Mr. de P. was back in his Stetson hat), we came to the dead smoky smell of old reefers and cartons of cigarette butts in ashtrays and nobody around but the dog. Romulus was lying in the middle of the floor with his diamond collar gone, and his throat cut. His eyes were open and he had the peculiar expression on his face of a young pup learning to sit on his hind legs. A simple dog look. Plus all that blood in the carpet which you couldn't see at first it was such a dark carpet.

Bobby started to blubber like a five-year-old kid. He cried and his belly shook a little and his big jaw looked really prominent the way a five-year-old kid with a big jaw can impress you with how mad they are going to be when they grow up. Then he came to a stop and knelt by the dog and got a little blood on his fingers and touched it to himself and to me, but so softly that I wasn't offended, as if that was a nice way to say goodbye to Romulus, and then we went back to the bedroom and made love which turned out to be sweeter than anything because it was full of sorrow, and I cried for the baby in my stomach who would soon be gone and the dead dog and for myself, and felt very sweet toward Bobby.

Later that day, I asked him, "Do you know who killed Romulus?" and he nodded.

I asked, "Are you going to do anything about it?"

"You bet," he said.

Bobby's father, I learned, had a very big automobile agency, whereas Bobby, who hated to work, had started an antique car offshoot and was good at it. He knew how to buy antique cars and sell them. Bobby had a boat that would "sleep six and do thirty-five knots" and he had ranch land in the Valley and his favorite horse, and three cars of his own, and I thought he was the wealthiest guy I'd ever met except for old Joe Schenck, who used to show me off to his friends at dinner. Before three days were gone, I decided that I wanted to marry Bobby and he was sure he wanted to marry me. The way he explained that he knew he was sure was that he hadn't made love to anybody, except at parties, for a long time, he said.

By the second full day we even went downstairs and I was introduced to his father and sister who both gave a look at me like "Fine, you're the one here for the week." Bobby never mentioned the dead dog and no one else did either. We would go for a drive in the afternoon, but most of the day and night each twenty-four hours was spent in bed. I never took so much marijuana ever. I didn't have a head any more, just a headache, and the most constant sexual desire I could hardly believe. At the studio where I used to take many more publicity shots than make real movies, the still photographers always used to act like I had so much sex I just had to squeeze it out of the tube. I always used to marvel at how sexy I could get myself to look, for I never felt a lot of what I used to show. In fact I used to worry if sexually speaking I was really a little constipated. But now it was the opposite. I felt like I was nothing but sex. Yet in the mirror I looked terrible. All tired and drawn and washed out. I was confused by the way my face always seemed to be one full step ahead or behind of me.

Then I began to have this ferocious headache. When we weren't making love, I felt nauseated and wondered if it was morning sickness, and slowly, day by day, more and more, Bobby de P. and me began to fight. Except they weren't quarrels so much as savage displays, you might say, of bad nerves, after which we'd be off once more. All the while we'd talk about getting married. Only it was like we were flipping a switch back and forth. Maybe it was the benzedrine. He kept feeding us pills until I couldn't sleep, and every time I came near to something fabulous, my chest also came near to exploding. Moreover, the pills made him bite me on the breast and other plump places. "What did you do with Rod?" he'd want to know. I'd tell him. He'd want every last detail. Then he would get excited.

On the fifth day Bobby said to me, "You want to get married?"

"Yes."

"Well, I'll get married."

"Let's," I said.

"We can't," he said. "I'm married already," and he bit me on the lip. I flung him off. "You said you were divorced."

"She won't give it."

His wife was living with Rod. Rod had killed the dog and then Rod stole the collar. Of course, that diamond collar used to belong to Bobby's wife but Bobby had taken it from her the day they broke up, and put it on the dog.

"Rod is away now," he said. "Rod is on location in Utah. Let's go over and visit my old lady."

"And tell her you want a divorce?"

He squeezed my arm so hard I could feel the bruise instantly. "No," he said, "we'll finish her off like the dog."

What I couldn't believe was the excitement it gave me. I was nearer to myself than I ever wanted to be. I remembered then what Abraham Robert Charles had said a few nights before, and I saw inside myself to the other soul, the one that never spoke. It was ready to think of murder. In truth, my headache went away. I tingled all over as I had on the motorcycle.

"Let's drive up to her house," he said. "I'll do it and you watch. Then we'll come back here. If we stick together, nobody can prove a thing. We can say we were in bed."

I could see us looking at each other forever, one year into the next. I could see my picture in the newspapers. "Starlet Questioned in Murder Case." The pictures would be printed in all the newspapers over the world. A candle could burn in a dark church at such a thought. The idea that everyone would talk of me was beautiful. Killing Bobby's wife almost felt comfortable. Maybe if I hadn't seen Romulus with that funny expression on his face where he was dead but still seemed to be learning to sit on his paws, maybe if I hadn't seen something in that animal lying there so calmly after his throat was cut, I might have worried about Bobby's wife, but now I just felt as if it was all fair somehow. Maybe Bobby would even let me keep the baby. I remember thinking of how I felt when I first saw my face on film in *Scudda-Hoo! Scudda-Hay!* and decided I was very interesting except I had what you might call a space, like Rod's, in my expression. There was something in me that didn't show itself to others. Like: I'm ready to commit murder.

We got into Bobby's car, and drove across Bel Air into Beverly Hills, and in one of the houses off Rodeo Drive was where she lived. It was dark, and there were no cars outside, and the garage was locked, so Bobby and I went to the back of the house. He found the wire to the burglar alarm and cut it and cracked the latch on the window. There we were standing in her kitchen. He looked in the rack for a carving knife and found one. Then we went up the stairs to her bedroom. I remember it was on the side that would have a view of the hills above Beverly Hills, and all the while he was doing this, despite the benzedrine in my blood, I never felt more calm as if, ha ha, I was on *This Is Your Life,* and they were talking about me looking for the woman's door. I even held Bobby's hand, the one that did not have the knife.

There was no lock to the master bedroom. By the light of the street lamps coming through the window, we could see that there was also no woman in the bed. The house was empty. We went through every room but it was empty. Bobby's wife must have gone on location with Rod.

We went home. Before the night was over, Bobby beat

me up, or at least he started to, but he was too drunk to catch me. I was awful sick of sex. I grabbed up my clothes and ran out the door and had the luck to find a taxi on those lonely streets and went home to Hollywood. I didn't even cry in the back seat. It just occurred to me that Bobby didn't know my phone number or my address, or even my last name, just my first, and maybe he would never try to find me, and he never did.

Two days later, I had the abortion. Whenever I looked into my mirror now in my apartment in the Waldorf Towers on the 37th floor, I could still see how something ended in me that day, I don't know what, but it is still in my expression.

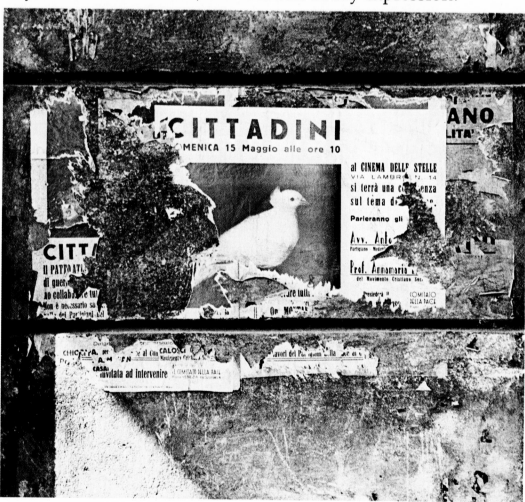

That first week at the Waldorf was when those particular memories came crawling in. I realized why I scream when I see cockroaches. It's because they look like the beginning of horrible thoughts. I certainly would turn away from the mirror, then. It would get too morbid. I watched TV instead, and on my black-and-white set everything looked like Seidlitz powders. I didn't like television because it made me want to burp. On the other hand, it was a little like having another person in the room. Nobody impressive, of course. Somebody who was pale and had a lot of stomach noises. Color TV was like they were putting makeup on that pale person. A very unhealthy person with a wheeze in their lungs and a twitch—if you got to know them well they would tell you about their operations. So I used to think TV was ridiculous. The entertainment industry, instead of understanding that they had this unhealthy individual who could only do a little bit, had it out instead working hard. Maybe one year it would come down with some awful disease, but in the meantime they were giving it dancing lessons.

Still, it was TV that allowed me to get my faith back in Milton. There were big offers coming in now for me to do dramatic parts on television, but Milton always said no, even though the Waldorf Towers was costing him $1,000 a week.

"You don't think I can act," I would tell him.

"I don't think TV can act," he would tell me back. "It's not for artists of stature like yourself." The way Milton said "artists of stature" made me understand that a little part of myself would always trust him completely. "I see nothing but heights for you," he added. "TV is the flats."

I was in such a peculiar situation. I was very much in love with Arthur Miller. In fact, before I left Connecticut, I had even told Milton I wanted to be in New York near the man I loved, all

143

the while knowing that Milton Greene had always supposed I was secretly in love with Milton Greene, but I was also beginning to understand that the more guys I got interested in for a day or two, like Marlon Brando, or Prince Rainier, the more I came back to thinking about Art, who had the perfect first name for a playwright as great as Arthur Miller, Art as in Great Art. I also used to call him AM because he liked to get up in the morning. Oh, Art, if he hadn't been so talented, he really could have worked for some big company and been out in the motel dining room for breakfast at 7 A.M. (good old Arthur Miller time) with his white shirt, his skinny tie, and his attaché case full of samples. Instead he was loaded with Art and I loved him.

Later, when Amy found out, she wanted to know how we met. I had wanted to keep Arthur Miller such a secret from her that I wouldn't even think about him in her presence. She was capable of looking up to say, "You're hiding a man from me." When Amy was just a baby in Cuba, she had been suckled by a witch, or at least that was what her family told her, and it must have gone right to her nose. Amy can smell the air, and watch out, your secrets are lost! I was glad, therefore, she found out finally. Then I could tell her how I ran into Art years ago before I even met Joe DiMaggio, and how it had been like a scene in a 20th Century-Fox movie musical, only better, because I had been all alone on the set of a sound stage. Since there was nobody else in the building, I was making believe that I was having a dance with Fred Astaire. In the middle of having this wonderful time with Mr. Astaire, I heard the door open. I shouldn't have been there, so I thought, it's the guard, I'll get thrown out. I hid behind some crates. Only it turned out to be two men who weren't guards, and one of them was a famous movie director named Elia Kazan and the other was Art. I didn't know what they were talking about, but I could hear them speaking, then all of a sudden I sneezed, which made them realize somebody was there. They must have wanted to be alone to have a private talk, because now they were upset. The shorter man, Kazan, came back and found me. There I was shivering behind a crate. "Who are you and what have you heard?" he wanted to know. I was practically whimpering telling him I didn't know anything. All the same, it turned out all right. I started having a little romance with Mr. Kazan, and we became good friends, which is what I mean, it doesn't always have to be horrible afterward. Anyway, Art was merely the shy guy in the background at the time. I knew he was a famous playwright, even though I'd never seen *Death of a Salesman*, but I had nothing really to do with him during that period. It was Elia "Gadge" Kazan I started seeing a little. But one night at a small party Mr. K. took me to a few weeks later, I happened to go out in the garden, and Mr. Miller and I started to talk, and I told him all about how I loved Abraham Lincoln and thought he was the greatest man who ever lived. All the while we were talking I noticed that AM certainly looked like Young Abe, and if AM had been an actor, and I was a casting director, I would have given him the role. To make it perfect he told me he had gone to Abraham Lincoln High School in Brooklyn. All the while we were talking—and it was for hours—he held my big toe. I felt like he was a gardener, and I was a beautiful flower. He was taking care of my roots. He had the nicest hand, a big hand, in which I could nestle my big toe, and in recollection it was like the way I felt later when I was up on the pink elephant. So I never forgot Arthur Miller. We would correspond and he would tell me to ignore the idea people had of me as a sexpot and realize I was a beautiful lady inside. I was happy to tell Amy all of this. I was relieved she finally knew. Because all the while I'd been living in Connecticut, I used to go into New York occasionally for the night, and spend it secretly with AM, then return to Connecticut next afternoon. I used to feel uncomfortable coming back in, like an alley cat out all night. I was dying to tell Amy about Mr. Miller, and how every moment away from Connecticut had been with him, I would have liked to say to Amy, "Arthur Miller is the gentleman I'm seeing, but you have to understand he's married and has children, and a home, and I am not a home-breaker." Only who would have believed the sincerity of my feeling? I used to know a lot of kids in foster homes, who were there because some woman had broken up their father and mother. Then the parents never got together again. For practical purposes, the kids were now orphans. So, one stigma I never wanted placed on me was that I deprived a child of its parents. Arthur would always explain to me that I was breaking up nothing. He and his wife had been ready to separate for years. I hoped it was true, and told myself it was, but I could not bring myself to tell Amy. Therefore I was relieved when she found out. Although it was crazy the way she did. One evening she and Milton were driving back from New York, and a bolt of lightning must have come from the witch that used to suckle her, because Amy said, "The fellow Marilyn's keeping company with is Arthur Miller." Milton almost ran off the road. Later when I asked her how she knew, she said it just came to her. When I talked about plays, or asked people if they'd seen this play or that play, I'd never say directly "What do you think of Arthur Miller?" Instead, I would mention Tennessee Williams and William Inge and only later intersperse Art's name. She thought that had something to do with the way she guessed.

Anyway, I felt good. I could bring my friends together now. So I told Mr. Miller that while I loved Brooklyn and adored walking through Brooklyn streets because those old brownstone buildings made me think of the Civil War and the Revolutionary

War inasmuch as Washington had crossed over from Brooklyn to New Jersey long before he ever had to look for the Delaware, I still wanted AM to meet some of my friends. So I told Amy, "I'll be out for the weekend, and Arthur is coming for Sunday brunch." Then I explained what I wanted Kitty to do in the way of preparation. I wanted a wonderful ham, a wonderful sweet-potato pie. I loved Kitty's sweet-potato pies, her deep-dish apple pie, and Amy said to me, "You're just a Jewish yenta. All you want is to give your man wonderful things to eat." The chicken in corn flakes, I told her, which was another absolutely marvelous thing Kitty made. And salad, and candied carrots, and a lot of good wine. I was so excited Arthur was coming and the house was shining, and filled with flowers.

I think he was a little nervous when he finally arrived. He talked a lot. In fact, Art talked the entire time. All those very funny stories, and I loved listening to him. But I knew Amy, who respected him immensely, wanted to get a word in edge-wise all the same, so I finally said, "Amy loved *Death of a Salesman*," which enabled her to tell the story of the night she saw it, and how everybody was so moved that no one clapped at the end. It would have been sacrilege to destroy what the audience felt, she said. Arthur said that that happened about once every ten days. It was the reaction he enjoyed most. Then we went in the living room and had coffee—Arthur was a big coffee drinker—and he talked about theater, and we all spoke about *Bus Stop*, which 20th Century wanted me to make if I was going to negotiate a new contract with them, and discussed whether Rock Hudson should play the lead opposite me, and after Arthur left, I wanted to know everything Amy thought about my man. She kept saying he was very nice. Only I didn't feel that little bit of true esteem running over. Two or three days later I said to Milton right in front of her, "Amy doesn't like Arthur," which made her say, "Listen, I have nothing against the man." That convinced me. I was right.

I didn't care. I was at the Waldorf now, and Art and I didn't have to walk for hours back and forth through Brooklyn and prove that love was not just sex, but the wonderful feeling you could get from looking at old buildings.

The next time Arthur and me got together with Amy and Milton was at Jimmy LaGrange's restaurant, which had a back room that was partitioned off for privacy. Everybody was real cool about it including the piano player, an awful nice man, and we arranged it so that Milton, Amy and myself would be there first and Art could slip in. "It's enough you're fighting Twentieth," Amy explained. "You don't have to be called a homewrecker as well."

In fact, we got so cautious that when *Cat on a Hot Tin Roof* opened, we all went as Tennessee's guests, but since I was going to be in a low-cut gown and all the photographers would be there, Arthur didn't even come in with us. We only joined up afterward at the opening-night party where I threw good old caution to the winds again and stayed by his side all night. In the sneakiest part of one of my two personalities, something must have been saying, "The hell with the bad publicity you're saving me from, what about all the good publicity I'm missing?"

The dark old water pump was working. Maybe ambition was also passionate. It certainly left me in a true state of excitement about Art and myself. Even the people who couldn't see straight when they heard my name would soon have to admit that this girl Marilyn Monroe was not merely an excuse for low sexual urges. After all, nobody in America was ever going to say that a gentleman like Arthur Miller with a face as full of character as his could be interested in the cheap side of sex. That was equal to saying Abraham Lincoln went around pinching girls on the QT. (Of course I was twenty-two years old before I realized that QT was not another name for your backside.) No, whether they liked it or not, a lot of prunefaces would soon have to say, "Marilyn Monroe must be more intelligent than I thought." I didn't understand, as yet, that people would say instead, "Arthur Miller has lost all good sense."

However, even if I wanted people to know of our romance, I had to be careful. With Arthur, you had to change one thing at a time. I figured his talent had to stay deep down. For that reason he did not like to add more than one factor to his life at a time. I could see this by how slowly he made friends with the Greenes.

Moreover, Art didn't really like Lee Strasberg. Now that I was in New York proper at the Waldorf, I was having the intellectual experience of my life learning how to act at Actors Studio. I would go there to witness various performances after studying in private with Mr. Strasberg, and no matter how much I had been taught about acting up to then, it was nothing compared to Lee because he got you scared of doing bad acting. He made you feel that if you were phony on stage there could be nothing worse. He was not a man whose looks most people liked right off, since he was short and very, what you might call, severe-looking—he always seemed to be smelling something stale in other people that he had to disapprove of. Yet he never looked that way at me. I believe something in his heart came to attention on the day we met, because I saw a jewel in his eye every time he stared in my direction. I think he believed that in my deepest parts there was nothing phony about me. That was the highest praise I could think of. All that year at the Waldorf, I felt like I was being watched over by three talented intelligent men (counting Milton) and on occasion, I really felt rosy. Milton even introduced me to Marlene Dietrich one day, and for a little while I felt just like her.

Now, Lee, that is, Mr. Strasberg, had a vocabulary a lot of people liked to make fun of. He used such words as "adjustment" and "contact" and "concentration" and they were hard to understand if you were not an actor. When it came to doing a part, I used to believe that if the role was good, it was actually living out there the way a spirit might be out there, except you didn't use a crystal ball to find the role, you made *contact*. You could sort of feel when you got into the person you were playing. It was more like the role came to you. In fact, it was awful trying to act if there was no contact. Except I could usually locate it. When you're able to mimic somebody you feel as if you are more entitled to their personality (even if it's President Eisenhower you're imitating) than they are. It's real contact. The only thing is, you have to keep it. For that you need concentration. Mr. Strasberg was a tiger about actors losing their concentration. After all, you might have to be in a role for twenty minutes, or even an hour if it's a long act, and you better have it. There are too many things on stage or in the audience that can break your contact.

For instance, you might be doing a character who is very much in love with one of the other characters on stage. But it so happens that the actor facing you is, as a human being, personally repulsive. Then you have to make an adjustment. It's no longer this particular human being you are talking to but someone imaginary in his place, someone who can bring out your good feelings. Only, for that, you need an awful lot of concentration. You have to be able to tell yourself, "It's really Arthur Miller I'm talking to right now, not this glob in front of me."

Anyway, all that winter and spring and summer I studied with Strasberg and sat in at Actors Studio. I saw a lot of actors there including Marlon Brando. Given the circumstances, Art wasn't able to see me every night, and there were occasions when I got depressed with the situation. It's not always nice to have a wonderful time with your guy and then know he's going home to his wife. So there were days when I knew I was going to be alone at night; and if Marlon would turn up at the Studio, for example, on such an afternoon, and say, "Want to go to dinner?" I would accept. Now, what we did after dinner was never planned nor need it ever be discussed. Whatever it was, I

keep it to myself. I did not get derailed from my romance with Art.

It was one year, I have to say, when my education was foremost. Not only had I learned a lot the winter before in Connecticut but Arthur kept bringing me literature—Russian books and Dostoevski—and we talked about my playing Grushenka someday. There were also a lot of pamphlets to read about the idea that the lower classes were at the behest of powerful forces if they didn't watch out. I could tell by Amy's expression when I spoke of all I was now learning that she thought I was being spoon-fed, but then, maybe I wanted to be. I could see all those Hollywood producers and executives as the upper classes loving to put their schmatte right under your nose. Myself I would picture as the proletariat. I liked the idea that the proletariat wouldn't have to owe nobody nothing in the future.

When she heard about this, Amy would fulminate, which is another word I learned and loved, *fulminate*. You could just see the fuse sparking. "Wait a minute," she'd say, "what is it you're telling me? I may have read one solitary book on Marx, and my one on Lenin, but this stuff is total fantasy and utopia. It can never be. Get it clear, Marilyn, there's an awful lot to love about this country." Of course, being from Cuba, Amy was a naturalized citizen, and you couldn't attack America around her. She'd want to kill. Once, when I said to her, "The working classes of the West will never buy the Cold War," she said, "What is that? Why are you saying that?"

"Arthur said it," I told her.

Amy said, "I don't give a shit what Arthur said." I couldn't believe it. Now Amy went out and bought me books about the Bill of Rights and the Declaration of Independence. Only, they were the kind of things you buy for age 14–16. I never forgave Amy. Meanwhile, it was useless to ask Milton about such things. When it came to politics he would get an expression on his face like he was one of the characters in *Alice in Wonderland.*

"Does it work?" he would ask in a hoarse voice.

"Does what work?"

"Does a horse gallop?"

Sometimes I thought Milton was even more ignorant than myself. At such times, I didn't know how he got his beautiful photographs.

"Listen," he would say, "it works. It stands up. Ignore it. You can't put a new pair of shoes on history."

Milton and Arthur were both from Brooklyn, but Arthur gave him a look like Milton was speaking Chinkey Chinese. "What is this dummy doing to the air?" would be Arthur's expression. And whenever Amy would try to argue, Arthur would get an even more pained expression. I used to think, "Amy, where do you get your crust? Art is a great playwright. They would give him all the prizes if they dared." Once I was coming into a room and actually heard Milton say to Amy from the other side of the door, "At the toll booth, he wouldn't even go for the dime." I knew he was talking about Arthur.

All the same, I was seeing a lot of Milton and Amy. When it was too lonesome at the Waldorf, I used to go back to Connecticut and spend a day or two with them, and many a night we went to the theater. *Bus Stop* we saw three times. On the first occasion, no sooner did the curtain come down than Milton said, "You are Cherie."

I really was close to offended. Cherie was the lowest sort of dumb roadhouse singer, except that this was legitimate Broadway and Miss Kim Stanley was doing it. She was awfully respected at Actors Studio and doing a wonderful job in front of me. Deep down, I wondered if I could ever act as well as her. So did I have the right to take her role?

Kim Stanley, Milton informed me, might not be as large an attraction as myself when it came to selling movie tickets. I didn't even have to ask myself the question, Milton said. I would certainly not be betraying her.

We went back to *Bus Stop*. Every time I got more confident. The leading man, Albert Salmi, was also from Actors Studio, and also wonderful. For me, Actors Studio was the equivalent of saying, "I went to Princeton." It showed. You know, "I'm a Harvard man. I'm supposed to run a bank." So it was with Actors Studio. "I'm supposed to be a mysterious and magnificent actor." Albert Salmi was truly in contact with his role. I began to itch to play it with him. While I still thought Kim Stanley was wonderful, I began to see where I could do certain things better. She played Cherie as a dumb girl whereas I would go out there and be dumb. Be the real article. There were a hundred kids in the orphanage I could make contact with.

 Milton told me I was going to meet Joshua Logan, the director of *Bus Stop*. Milton began talking of a package for Twentieth, but I kept saying, "Josh Logan, I don't think I can meet him. I mean, the man won't see me. Why should he see me?" I kept thinking, "Josh Logan did *Mr. Roberts* and *South Pacific*. What would he care about me?" Milton said that Josh Logan felt the same. He hadn't directed any movies yet. So he was thrilled that I would see *him*! I didn't believe it. Milton was like one of those Arabs who can sell you a carpet right in the street, they have such nice eyes. Yet, when I met Mr. Logan and his wife, Nedda, they were very gracious. Oh, I was in love with the New York theater. I even did *Anna Christie* with Maureen Stapleton at the Studio, the hardest single thing I did in my life, and the day of

it, and the night before, was the worst ever. I felt as if I didn't have a skin. When I played it, all my feelings were exposed. I might as well have been the widow at the funeral. Even saying hello to people could prove a catastrophe. You'd never stop crying. However, I got through it, and people said it was extraordinary. Lee Strasberg even told Josh Logan that I and Marlon Brando were the two finest film stars with whose work he was familiar, and of the two, I was even finer. (How I hoped Marlon would hear that. It would change his day.)

So everything could have been wonderful, except the next morning, right after *Anna Christie*, I had laryngitis. What if I had to give a performance tonight? The more Lee talked of my becoming a Broadway actress, the more I knew that one of the two people in me (one of them at least) was going to expire if I gave up being a movie star. Maybe it was the two of them. After all, why could I not speak today at all, so to speak?

Meanwhile, Milton was short of money. It was close to something awful by now. All the same he kept paying my bills, and I would hear him on the telephone keeping up a big front with Twentieth. It even looked like they were coming around to what Milton said would be a fabulous improvement in my contract.

Instead of getting $700 a week every week of the year, I would now get $100,000 for each movie I did for them and would only have to do four movies in seven years. In the time between, I could do pictures for myself, that is, for Marilyn Monroe Productions. I could also pick my director for each 20th Century-Fox film. There was a special list of sixteen we agreed on: George Cukor, John Ford, Alfred Hitchcock, John Huston, Elia Kazan, David Lean, Joshua Logan, Joseph Mankiewicz, Vincente Minnelli (but only for musicals), Carol Reed, Vittorio de Sica, George Stevens, Lee Strasberg, Billy Wilder, William Wyler and

Fred Zinnemann. (For a moment I wanted to call Joe DiMaggio because that sort of thing might impress him. It was like an All-Star team.)

Later I learned that it was a very close call financially speaking for Milton. We did, however, sign the contract right after the first of the year, January 4, 1956, and Milton said, "This will be the big year for you." It was. In fact, soon as he had the contract, Milton was able to borrow the money to buy a play called *The Sleeping Prince*, by Terence Rattigan. Milton told me, "We'll do it with Olivier. Monroe and Olivier is a combination nobody can ignore. *The Prince and the Showgirl* we'll call it."

Then we had a small misunderstanding. One of the small but fatal kind. I mentioned to Lee Strasberg how Milton thought Olivier was a possibility to be not only the actor in our new movie but the director. Lee said, "It might be a good idea." So I told Milton, who immediately sent an offer and Olivier accepted both jobs. Right afterward, I learned that Lee had really wanted to discuss the thing a little further. "It *might* be a good idea." Sir Laurence Olivier was going to have different opinions about acting than the ones Lee had been instructing me in.

"Marilyn, you got to go with the telegram," Milton said. "We can't tell Olivier, 'Take off your hat. You're no longer the director.'"

I didn't know if I liked it. Milton, maybe, had maneuvered the whole thing through. I started to say something, but Milton said, "This picture will take you out of being a sexpot forever." Then he told me Warners had already agreed to finance it. He was proud of the deal. "I told Lou Wasserman, 'No interest.' He said, 'What? It's never been done!' 'Lou,' I told him, 'no interest.' Marilyn, this is the only film I know that is being financed with no interest."

I tried to understand. If I was getting educated in a lot of new ways, then maybe I should try to understand business as well. But I couldn't. I always felt it was not high finance but wealth that beautiful women should have a feeling for.

Then Olivier and Terence Rattigan came to New York from London. I didn't know if I felt comfortable with them. It was like talking to two dukes. They were so well-bred you couldn't tell the difference between real men and not. It was all dear boy. Except I thought Olivier was made of steel.

At our press conference to announce the film, there was pandemonium at the Plaza Hotel. I hadn't had a press conference in a long time, and I could see Mr. Olivier thought it was a zoo. He not only had an iron hand but an iron butt.

I was embarrassed. Most of the questions kept coming my way. I wanted to tell the press, "Don't you understand that Sir Laurence Olivier is the most distinguished star of stage and screen?" but I didn't dare. There could always be a slip-up with reporters.

Then Olivier said, "Miss Monroe has the extremely extraordinary gift of being able to suggest one moment that she is the naughtiest little thing, and the next that she's perfectly innocent."

When he said that, my eyes started to smart, and my feelings were definitely hurt. I felt I was on the auction block and being sold to another foster home. All the same, so soon as the press cheered (and, boy, were their foreheads shiny from sweating in the hot lights!) I began to move in my chair. Simply couldn't help it. Those bright lights brought out the worst. I was wearing a black silk camisole top with little tiny black spaghetti straps, and a black velvet jacket with a sable collar. It was so hot I immediately took off the jacket. Then I popped one shoulder higher, then the other.

"What would you like to do next, Miss Monroe?"

3161-1A
2L
3161-6J
3161-1B
4B
6K
1C
4G
6L
1D
4H
6M
KODAK SAFETY FILM

"Grushenka. That's from Dostoevski."

"Spell it for us."

"Begins with a G, I think." Soon as I said that, my shoulders rotated, and I gave another pop of my arm as if to say, "Let me hide behind my sweet juicy shoulder," but what popped was my shoulder strap. You would have thought the press were cannibals. They climbed over each other's ears to get an extra look. It was as if one look at my bare bosom would keep them alive for a year. Of such is human flesh. I didn't even show that much, just a little more of what they had been studying already. But I could see a thin line wrinkle up between Sir Laurence Olivier's eyes. God Save the Queen.

 After the press conference, I could see that Sir Laurence Olivier was annoyed. It's terrible being the Number Two actor anywhere. "Oh, yes," they say, "you were good, too." You feel like the younger kid in a family that's put its hopes on the older one. I knew Sir Laurence wasn't used to that but, I thought, "Well, competition never hurt anybody." Which was definitely one of Amy's ideas, not Arthur's.

All the same, Olivier and I started to have some fun. On nights when Arthur wasn't along, we'd flirt. Nothing to cause a scandal, but I never had such fun. Royalty knew how.

"My dear," Sir Laurence would say, "if ever I meet anyone as beautiful as you again, I shall collapse. It will all cave in."

"The breastworks and the earthworks," I said back to him. It was as if they'd painted my mind with silver. I would feel so bright around Olivier that I didn't even know how the words came to me.

"Yes. You're the most beautiful woman I've ever seen," he said. Then he shook his head. "No, you would be," he remarked, "but the tip of your nose is funny."

I slapped his hand. He loved to give it and to take it back. I bet the English think twice about lending each other their sexual organs. Now we started lighting each other's cigarettes. First I'd do his, then he'd leap up for mine. "Oh, your glass is empty," he'd say and call out, "Champagne for Miss Monroe." "My God," I'd say to myself, "it's *Olivier!*" Amy was totally in love with him. With all this gallantry, I even had the feeling Arthur was getting jealous, but I couldn't tell. When Art was with us, he had his head in the clouds, and his mind down in the deep thoughts. I could see it bothered him that the upper classes were so charming. "Let's not talk politics," said Olivier. "All those men of the left and the right are alike. Swine is swine."

At separate times, Arthur and Lee Strasberg were explaining to me not to be too impressed with Sir Laurence Olivier. At this point in his career, they said, he needed a new image. Someone like me to be associated with. Yet I couldn't help it. Sir Iron-Butt was a little like God to me. He was so funny. One day in the restaurant they brought him a lobster that only had one claw. The waiter explained that the shellfish were savage and fought in the tank.

"Not good enough," Olivier told him. "Remove this fellow and bring me the winner."

When the waiter left, Sir Laurence winked at all of us and said, "The remark comes from Feydeau."

"Plato?" I asked.

"Do-play or don't-play," said Larry, "but pronounce your names properly, you poop."

I couldn't stop giggling until I realized Arthur was about ready to frown his face off.

Sir Laurence Olivier toasted me. "To be beautiful! What

power! What good fortune! To see everyone bowing to your beauty with as much respect as is paid to a great man!" I nodded. I wished I could feel like a great man instead of a cat who was caked in powder. "Yes," said Sir Laurence, "it was Providence that wrote your beauty on your brow. That is the most glorious power," he said, looking into my eyes, "if only you know how to use it."

"Did you just make that up?" I asked him.

"Of course not. An actor can only speak in the words of others."

"Arthur can speak in his own words," I said.

"Arthur is blessed," said Olivier.

One night, we went to see *The Diary of Anne Frank* with Lee's daughter, Susan Strasberg. Naturally I was so involved with Lee and his wife Paula that I was pulling for Susan like I was also in the family. By the time the performance was over, I'd been sending so many nice thoughts her way that I felt tired. I thought she'd done a very good job. I said so to Olivier. "Good but limited," he remarked. I knew he couldn't stand the Strasbergs. "So much of this murky stuff is intolerable," he said to Arthur and to me. "They make too much of what they feel inside. Acting may be an animal instinct, but you want the animal trained. You certainly don't want the beast biting its own leg. I say: Learn the words, and then go out and do your job. Because that is your job. Either you're an actor or you're not. If you are not, *please*, be a plumber, but leave me alone." Arthur nodded wisely. "I don't know that I disagree with you." At present, Lee Strasberg had a great deal of reputation in the theater, Arthur Miller said, but there was something secretive about what he was purveying. "Acting is communication," Arthur said.

"Well, I don't agree," I told them. I felt like they were just chipping away at everything.

"Darling," said Sir Laurence, "a good actor has to strike his own note. Elegance, after all, is built on the idea that you must choose. You simply cannot order every dessert." Something in the way he said it had me near to fainting. It was the idea that there was one dessert worth all the others. I wondered why it was my luck that whenever I got really near to being absolutely wild about Art, some prince like Olivier always had to come my way. Now Amy began to lecture me across the table, right in front of Arthur. Certain people had the misfortune, she said, of having to live without enough to eat. That was unspeakable. But after all, people with money also knew unhappiness. You could make a bad choice between two exciting possibilities and take the wrong road. "Marilyn," she told me, "realize that you live in this second kind of world."

I knew that was why Amy didn't like Art. AM still acted as if the world where everybody was hungry happened to be the only world there was. "Maybe," I said to myself, "that's why I love him. He understands me better than Amy ever could, or Sir Larry. He knows I always feel hungry inside."

Still, I loved being with Olivier. He told such wonderful stories. They were like chapters out of the books I used to read in Connecticut. There was one about a woman named Lola Montez that even gave me dreams. Lola Montez once met a mad king named Ludwig of Bavaria (Ludwig!), and he said her breasts were so beautiful they couldn't be real. Just had to be an example of the art of the corsetmaker. Well, Lola Montez picked up a letter opener from King Ludwig's writing desk and ripped her dress down the middle right there in front of him. I could see myself doing the same scene with Larry Olivier. "Do you know," I said, to change the subject, "maybe eating is like fancy chairs. I've been looking in the Museum at Dutch chairs and French chairs with Milton, and I think the Dutch just like to be

164

there." "Whatever do you mean?" Sir Larry asked. "Well, it's as if the Dutch said: Let the chair take care of your weight, but the French put inlaid woods in the back and they used silk fabrics that are so delicate a person with a heavy behind could split the cloth. I guess what they're saying is that the chair comes first. If your bottom is too big, forget it—don't sit down! I think the French like to put in a lot of work where no one else would bother. Isn't that elegance?"

"Yes," he said. "In fact, my dear, it's rather well put."

"Well," said I, "that's what we do at Actors Studio. Put in a lot of work where no one else would bother."

I could see Arthur looking at me with a glint, and Amy threw up an arm like she was giving the ears of the bull. That night when we got home, Arthur said he had come to a conclusion that he was going to get a divorce. While I was making *Bus Stop*, he would go out to Reno and obtain it. So before we said goodbye to Sir Laurence, and he went back to London, I said to Milton, "Make sure you're paying him enough. Give Sir Laurence what he wants. Don't be cheap."

"Marilyn," said Milton, "I'm giving him more than he wants. There's a reason."

"You just don't be cheap," I said.

"No, Marilyn," said Milton, "I'm giving him more than he's asking. Because once your picture starts, he's going to find out."

Paula Strasberg came along as my personal dramatic coach for the shooting of *Bus Stop*. She was small and dumpy, and that was her bad luck, but it was also her good luck to know that nobody was going to pretend to like her unless they did. As a result, she didn't waste time trying to get along with everybody. She just worked for you.

Whereas, Natasha Lytess, who used to be my dramatic coach when the studio was just beginning to give me roles, was always very jealous of who I saw when I'd go out by myself, at least when I used to live with Natasha, right after Bobby de P. and before Joe D. She'd practically be my husband. Let's not get into it.

Now I was going to make a movie without her. When I arrived in Los Angeles, Natasha was saying to the papers that she didn't understand how I could afford to fire her. I needed her services, she said, like "a dead man needs a coffin." I didn't like that. She was practically calling me a witch. It certainly made everybody on the set pay more attention to Paula and me between takes, and cause them to wonder what we said.

I was glad people didn't know. Sometimes, in the breaks, Paula would whisper, "Be a bird," or "Be a tree." It was a way to tell you what colors to add to what you were doing. If I was too solemn, for instance, she wouldn't say, "Don't be so serious," she'd say, "Be a bird." That way I would try to feel light. If she wanted me to stand up for myself in a scene and let nothing sway me too far, she'd whisper, "Be a tree."

But what would have driven them crazy, if they could have heard, was "Be an oil painting." Or "Be a watercolor." That sort of instruction really worked. When I tried to be an oil painting, I felt significant inside. Whereas with a watercolor, I could get as ripply as a brook.

"Terrific," Josh Logan would say.

Milton had done the costumes and selected a wonderful white makeup for me. Cherie was a girl who never saw the sun. In addition, Josh Logan was considerate most of the time, so it wasn't too terrible a movie to make. Except I hated Don Murray, who played opposite me. I had to make an adjustment to him all the time. "I wipe you out," I kept saying to myself, "you're someone else." Who he was, depended. I hate to say it, but once I even made him Rod, the stunt man. That was in order to get myself feeling, "Oh, well, willing or not, ready or not, he's an attraction."

On the other hand, while we were in Los Angeles, I lived with Milton and Amy and Josh in a large house we rented in Beverly Glen, and Amy went over the lines with me every night. That made me feel well prepared so far as the script was concerned, and Paula seemed to know just the right exercise to select to help me make contact with Cherie again. "You're a leaf and the wind is blowing you."

It was just that something spooky began to take place. I did not know how to explain it to anyone. The better I made contact, the more exhausted I felt when the day was over. After a while I began to feel as if Cherie was truly out there, that she was someone who'd really lived and died and then got the ear of Mr. William Inge so she could become a character in his play. Now, when I made contact with her, it felt like I was not only living my own life but her old one as well. If you were a secretary and had to work all day, of course you'd be tired. But if you had to do your job and also do the job for the girl at the next desk, you would be worn out. The longer I worked on *Bus Stop,* the more screwed tight I would get until I couldn't relax enough to play the scene unless I slipped down a couple of Seconal each night. That left me stupid and funny next morning. I finally got bronchitis and lost a full week on the set, so by the time we finished, I knew Mr. Logan was ready to breathe one whew of relief. I felt sordid. I never wanted to see Cherie again, yet everybody was telling me it was the best role I'd ever done. I couldn't even stand her stupid face. I felt like I'd been living in a terrible dumb person.

 All the while I was thinking about getting married. AM had stayed in Reno and out at Pyramid Lake, Nevada, writing short stories while waiting for his divorce. On weekends he would slip into L.A. and we would share an apartment at the Château Marmont. It drove Milton crazy. Because on Monday I wouldn't always be on time for work. Art and I would stay up late and I would drink so I could unwind. After the weekend, Milton would greet me on Monday with a doctor and a B$_{12}$ shot. Then

he would scold me for putting on weight. I would say, "None of your business. It's personal."

Milton would say, "I'd like to talk to Arthur. We're making a film."

"None of your business," I'd say. I was hurt when I found out that Milton had made two complete sets of costumes for me. One was larger, and to be used only on Monday morning. Bloated, I guess Milton would say. I rushed back to New York as soon as the film was done. Another week and my entire nervous system would have been in jeopardy. I could feel it.

I loved Arthur because he seemed to know the answer to everything, and when he didn't, why then this wonderful sadness would come off him and he would brood. He didn't always understand what bothered me, but he made the effort, and that was so attractive. Nobody had ever worried as much about my feelings as Arthur. Milton sometimes knew just what to do for them, but Arthur did the worrying. Of course, twice a year when I was ready to give it all up, Milton would say, "Chaplin. You will be in white, and Charlie Chaplin will be in black." That was all I needed. I knew if I ever got together with Mr. Chaplin there would be no need for contact in any role—I would just react to Charlie Chaplin. Acting would be as simple as Ping-Pong. So I loved Milton for knowing when to say that. Milton would help me then in a way Arthur never could, but, oh, I was so mad about AM. When I saw *Death of a Salesman*, I thought it was the greatest play I ever went to, greater than Shakespeare, and here was this tall skinny forty-year-old fellow in my room talking like a boy with a big grin at how funny the world was, yes, Art had these two speeds, brooding and funny, and I loved them both. A lot of the time he was so tender I didn't think of it as sex any longer but mighty like a rose, what a wonderful song that was. I could tell him in all honesty, "It was never so perfect before." Not a ghost to haunt me as I said it.

We had a real problem, though. The State Department wouldn't give Art a passport to accompany me to England for *The Prince and the Showgirl*. They practically said it was due to Communist leanings. Chairman Walter of the House Un-American Activities Committee wanted Arthur to testify in Washington. We heard that if he refused to talk they could give him a year in jail. I couldn't have been more full of worry when we went to Washington for the hearing, and I never felt closer to

Art. It was us against the world. That is the most beautiful feeling you can have, and Arthur told them the next day in Congress that he wanted to go to England to be with the woman "who will then be my wife." He held my earrings in his hands as he said it, and I thought he sure wanted to be in England, what with Olivier there, and almost got the giggles at the thought but fought them back. It made me realize that I had to concentrate just as much in my life as my work to keep those loose nuts from rattling.

In the next day or two, editorials started being written all over the world to complain about America's treatment of one of her leading artists. That must have made the State Department give in. They soon passed the word, "Give Miller a passport. Regardless of his politics." To which I wished to add, "Yes, isn't this a democracy?"

Now there was a rush to get married. Outside our apartment in New York, reporters were camped up and down the street. Every time we went out, they chased us in their cars. They wanted an announcement of the wedding. Arthur and I stood on the sidewalk at 57th Street and he told them we would give a press conference on Friday in Roxbury, Connecticut, where he had his home. I could see a look in Arthur's eye. He was accustomed to little press conferences, one or two reporters, maybe three, who would ask him respectful questions and really want to hear what he said. But Arthur wasn't used to being with a rude bunch like this. He was learning how they only wanted to prod you to say something idiotic for their headline.

They made so much pressure that on the drive up to Roxbury on Friday there was an accident. Before it happened, I even felt the air getting heavy. A woman from *Paris-Match* was chasing us, and her car went off the road on a turn. She got thrown out and killed. Worst of all, we were only a couple of hundred yards from the house—one more turn and she would have been alive. So when I saw her, I couldn't keep control of myself. Being on the front page all week gave me the same taste of pennies on my tongue that I used to feel after seeing Mr. Farnsworth—all used up! Now, here was the dead girl looking like Romulus. That same pool of blood. That same special look. As if she was awaiting instructions.

When we walked up to the house, I felt a terrible panic. Like the wedding was doomed. "Let's do it tonight," I said, and Arthur agreed. Therefore, on the drive back to New York, we did it with a judge in the White Plains courthouse.

But Sunday we had the real wedding. It was with a rabbi at Arthur's agent's house, Kay Brown, in Katonah, and that was more in the nature of a real one. In fact, we worked like crazy to get ready for it. There were a lot of problems, especially about clothes. Arthur did not have a black suit. The most he'd ever wear to get dressed up was slacks and a jacket, or chinos and a tweed jacket. Maybe he owned a navy-blue suit. But he was not what you'd call a snappy dresser. So I asked Milton to ring somebody up for help, and a friend of his brought over six suits to choose from. They got Arthur outfitted from top to toe. Meanwhile John Moore and Norman Norell were doing the same for me. I wanted white, only Amy said, "You can't wear it. You have to go for beige, you've been there already." I could have cried. I wanted white. I wanted to carry lilies and wear a long veil. "Don't you understand," I wanted to say to Amy, "I am *really* getting married for the first time? Do not tell me I've been there before." "No," said Amy, looking at me, "white would be tacky. You'll be lovely in beige. Dress in the color of champagne." That cheered me up. Champagne in a shiny slippery satin. We would have a beige chiffon, said Norman Norell, with a very plain neckline, little snug sleeves. For something borrowed, I would wear Amy's wedding veil. Three beautiful round pieces of veiling, one right on top of the other. It was white, but Norman Norell took it away with Amy and they dyed it in tea and it came out champagne. So I told myself that secretly I was still wearing white. Then Amy brought in parchment hose from Bendel's, the only place to sell stockings that color, and I got all dressed up, and the Strasbergs were there and the Rostens and a few of our other friends, and practically none of the press, thank God we fooled them. I went to the bedroom with Milton and Lee and Amy for a quiet moment before the ceremony, but that dead girl was still very much in my mind and I said, "Tell me if I'm making a mistake. Tell me if you don't want me to do it. If you say it's wrong, I won't do it." Milton looked at me and began to shake. "I can't do that," he said. "You have to tell me if you really don't want to. You have to say . . ." He shook his head, he started to stutter. "It's a major step," he finally said. Lee Strasberg just stood there not saying a word, and I thought to myself, "None of it feels real. I'm playing a role that I'm deeply in love with Arthur Miller, and my concentration has been superb until this moment. But now I've lost contact with the part. Milton is really saying to me, 'Tell us that you don't want to get married, and we'll take you away!'" I looked at him a long time. I thought about it. We didn't sneeze, we didn't breathe.

I began to think of how I had converted to Judaism and had to study the Old Testament with a rabbi, then of how I met Arthur Miller's folks and loved them very much, his father, Isadore, and his mother, Celia. Amy was able to help me with the Old Testament because she had converted long ago when she married Milton. Mrs. Miller had begun to teach me how to prepare gefilte fish, and chopped liver and chicken soup with matzoh balls plus other things like borscht. I looked at Lee and Milton and Amy and thought, "What am I an actress for, anyway?" So I smiled, very cynically, I suppose it looked, and I said, "Oh, what the hell, we can't disappoint the guests," and Amy spoke up in her big voice and said, "My God, doomed before they even take the vow!" and we all laughed, since that was one line from *My Fair Lady* that Amy and I were awful fond of, in fact the very words Professor Higgins used when Liza was

going to marry Freddy Eynsford-Hill. Now Lee said, "Yes or no?" and I took Amy's hand and said, "OK, go out and light the candles, and tell everybody we'll be there."

Lee Strasberg acted like my father and gave me away and Hedda Rosten and Judy Kantor and Amy were the bridesmaids, or really the matrons of honor, all dressed in sandy, soft-colored things, and a rabbi gave the service, and before you knew it, Arthur forgot to stomp on the glass, and Milton stepped on it instead, and crushed it, and everybody yelled Mazel Tov, and Arthur turned and kissed me. Later, Amy told me that in her wedding, she and Milton were married on the lawn and the damned glass wouldn't break cause the ground was too soft underneath, so maybe Milton felt like destiny owed him one glass, and he cracked mine.

 The day after the wedding I realized that when I asked Milton if I should get married I was playing nothing but a scene. After all, I had been married already on Friday night by the Judge. I just hadn't felt married.

Now, I did. Art and I stayed in Roxbury for a week. I watched the bumblebees fly up to the flowers near the front porch, and had funny thoughts such as that the bees are to nature what the press is to me. I giggled at the idea of reporters taking all my honey, and then got mad at the thought as well. Really, that was how I often felt—like a flower without honey —just green and damp and bitter inside.

Art kind of collapsed that first week. We were happy but we were also like two orphans in a storm. We held onto each other and felt very tired. I realized that in his own way Art was almost as delicate as me, and things took a lot out of him. I decided then that he wouldn't be able to take care of me quite as

much as I had expected. He might turn out to be more of a hitching post than a house with four walls. Still, that made me love him more than ever. It was so unexpected to think maybe he needed me too. I mean, Art had such a strong face. It was a new understanding for me to see that when there was a lot of terrible tension from events, and his emotions were all in an uproar, the only way it showed was that his jaw muscles got tighter, and his skin turned yellow under the tan. Considering that he was such a nice sensitive fine Jewish man, Art reacted a little bit like the Mafia, physically speaking.

We needed more time than that week. I just wanted to watch the bumblebees buzz around the flowers. So we cabled Milton, who was already in England for the Olivier movie, and told him we'd like another ten days. He sent back a telegram to tell us that the production would lose a lot of crucial time. "You can have a wonderful honeymoon right here in England, Larry Olivier says."

We had to go, therefore. But we were angry. For the first time, I felt ready to despise Milton Greene. It came over me all over again that he had broken my glass at the wedding. That was not humorous but . . . I asked Art for the word. "Preemptive," he said.

I had something like thirty pieces of luggage. Art had two or three. I liked that. I would have hated a husband with as much luggage as me. On the other hand, we learned at the airport that the overweight was going to cost a thousand dollars additional. I was ashamed of the amount. I still thought a thousand dollars was something you could buy a new car with.

There were a lot of newspapermen at Idlewild and I told them how happy I was to be working with Laurence Olivier.

Arthur made the mistake of saying we needed peace, rest, private and quiecy. That is, he didn't say that, but it was what I heard instead of quiet and privacy, and I got a round, blank look on my face trying not to laugh, which unfortunately was what they photographed. So I came out like the top crust in a pie before it goes in the oven. Then, Arthur had to say that living with me was like being a fish in a bowl. Also a big mistake. They picked a picture of him with his eyes protruding.

Laurence Olivier came to greet us at the airport with his wife, Vivien Leigh, and she hated me on sight. I thought she had a right to. She had played my part on the stage. Now I was playing her part in the movie. With her husband.

"Oh, do the newspapers always treat you this way?" she asked.

"Usually it's a little more," I said. Her nose went in the air.

 We had a big house in Eggham called a cottage, and the Oliviers were about an hour away at their place called Notley Abbey. I expected to see a couple of monks standing around being butlers, but didn't voice my expectations, ha, ha. After we were there a couple of days, but still not used to the change in time, Sir Laurence and Lady Olivier gave a big dinner party for us at Terence Rattigan's house. Amy called and was very excited about it. "Everybody in England will be there, my darling," she said. My heart sank. Everybody who was curious about Arthur and me. It would be like a slave auction. "Look at their teeth."

"It's going to be wonderful," Amy promised me.

Arthur reminded me that he didn't have a dress suit. That made me realize I wasn't sure what I wanted to wear. "Tell me the dress to put on?" I asked Amy over the phone. She said,

"What are you talking about? You've got wonderful things."
"Don't want to wear them," I said. "I don't have anything to wear." I had spent a couple of hours thinking of each one of my dresses and how those women in England were going to look at them. "That slave girl doesn't carry her clothes right," they'd say. "My God, darling," Amy told me, "this is three hours before the party." She sounded—to use her word—vexed. Milton had bought me a lot of things, after all. "You've got to help me," I said. "I don't know what to put on." "Well—" she took a deep breath—"why don't you wear the white dress you're going to be in for the movie? Have the hairdresser fix you a perfect Edwardian upsweep." She was right. She was always right. Now, it was just a question of Arthur. He decided to wear the black suit he got married in, but didn't have a bow tie. Of course, I didn't mind him in a string tie. I knew Amy would think he looked like Abraham Lincoln's poor cousin, but then I was tired of seeing things through Amy's mind.

The party was exactly what I expected. All the gentlemen wore impeccable dinner jackets and the women had gotten their jewelry and put it on. I wished I had a maid like La Belle Otero. And some jewelry. At the party, Amy kept saying, "What a nice gesture for the Oliviers to make," but I didn't think so. I had never seen so many fancy people in my life. Their way of talking froze my vocal cords. I couldn't get a word out. "Darling Marilyn," Olivier would say, "I want you to meet Sir Lord Rumpty-dump," and there would be a man who looked like a British colonel in a Hollywood movie with a monocle and a sash around his waist. He would bow and I would say "How do you do?" and keep talking to Arthur. Milton grabbed me for a dance. "What's the matter with you?" he asked. "What are you doing this for? You know these people are being very nice." "Shut your mouth, Milton," I told him, "you made Art and me get

here a week early." I felt a terrible temper building towards Milton, so I made a point when we sat down at the table to invite Arthur to sit next to me. Olivier was on my left. And Arthur was supposed to sit on Vivien Leigh's right. But he didn't. We even changed the place cards. And I made a point of talking to Arthur much more than to Larry through the meal. Only I couldn't keep ignoring him. I think that was because I had started to brood about diamonds. All the while Arthur was telling me funny things about the class system in England (in a low voice, of course) I was simply brooding about diamonds. I had seen so many of them tonight I'd gotten to know them better. I was ready to bet that diamonds brought light to you direct from the stars. That was why people wanted them, because it put you in touch with far-off places. "Did you ever hear," I asked Olivier, "of Robert de Montesquiou?" "Who?" he asked. I tried to pronounce it and then finally had to spell it. "Oh," he said, "de-mon-tes-qui-*ou*" as if there was only one way to pronounce it in all the world. "Oh, yes, of course I know de Montesqui*ou*. He's the Baron de Charlus. In fact, my dear, Montesquiou once made a remark that is commonly attributed to Oscar Wilde. 'However amusing it may be to speak ill of one's enemies, it is even more delectable to speak ill of one's friends.' "

Well, I was all ready to speak ill of Larry Olivier's friends. The books at Amy's house had described how the little-tittied women of England 100 and 200 years ago used to have fake bosoms made for them from wax. Then, they'd cover their chest with a veil. It must have looked like wax fruit. I could notice a couple of ladies around right now who looked like they were up to something of the same. They all had their noses high in the air. I could see why. English ladies had these bumps in the bridge, together with a lot of little indentations in the tip. It was

as if they didn't want to be caught short with a blunt instrument like mine. Of course, that still didn't keep them from hanky-panky. Why, even back in 1750, the ladies used to go to massage parlors and sit inside a special overcoat as large as a tent. This overcoat had a lot of sleeves into which the massage boy could put his arms. Then his hand would massage the ladies' bare bodies. Of course he couldn't see what he was doing, but, oh, what a good lathering for everybody. I was ready to tell Arthur about it, only that wasn't the sort of story to amuse him right now. So I turned once more to Sir Laurence at my left, and said, even though I didn't want to, "It's an elegant party, Larry."

"Oh, bloody all on elegance," he said. He was a little drunk. "All this is something you buy off a rack. Want to hear about the real article?" I nodded.

"Well, there used to be a fellow who went into Tortoni's in Paris around the turn of the century. He would order a vanilla ice-cream ball and a strawberry ice-cream ball. They had to be on separate plates, mind you. Then he would take off his brogans, and slip the vanilla into the right shoe and the strawberry into the left. Then he would put them on and walk out. Now, that, Marilyn, is elegance."

Arthur said, "Let's dance." We did a lot that night. Arthur had learned how in Brooklyn, and the best kind of dancing he did was dirty dips. At the end of every whoop-de-doo in the fox-trot, down we would go into a dip. He had the longest leg. Then he would come up with his leg in the air. If you weren't careful, you could look like he had left you on a clothesline. As we passed Amy, however, he started dancing in circles and she called out, "Arthur, that's a stellar twirl."

I was glad to sit down. I did not like the way those English ladies were looking at me and Arthur dance. I could practically read their lips. They had to be saying, "This is one actress who would rather do her performing on a mattress." It was a remark to stab you through the heart.

At the end of dinner, I didn't talk to Larry any more. He made a point of tapping me on the shoulder. He said, "Here's a good story about de Montesquiou. A cousin of his decided to marry completely beneath herself. He told her, 'One month of happiness, then forty years at the end of the table.'" Those words succeeded in completely ruining the evening for me.

As we left I could see the expression on Amy's face. Her eyes were saying, "That's Arthur for you. If he isn't controlling the environment, he's miserable."

We weren't on the movie two days before I was unhappy. I usually don't know how things are going for me, personally, so I need someone like Paula Strasberg to point me in the right direction. On the other hand, I can always tell when the chief is headed for disaster. So I began to worry about what the world's greatest actor was doing to this picture as a director. I was playing an American music-hall girl on tour in Europe, and he was playing a Balkan prince who was visiting London for the marriage of Prince George and Princess Mary. "Pure turn of the century," said Sir Laurence to the crew, as if being British they need know no more. Sir Laurence Olivier was so good that he could shift his posture and immediately switch the year. Right now, he was playing a perfect prince, stiff as steel. He sounded like he learned German with a Bulgarian accent, and then picked up his English with a German-Bulgarian accent. It was like Sir Laurence Olivier would start with a mark of 99 and then worry about getting 100. I never acted before with somebody who was so perfect in their role. He didn't seem to know about other actors having trouble with contact. Why, as the director, he would talk to the cameraman, then light a cigarette. Presto, he

was the Prince. I couldn't believe it. I had to concentrate for hours just to get near Elsie, who I was playing, and Elsie was a lot like me in the first place.

In that sense, if that's what acting was, Sir Laurence Olivier was the world's greatest actor. He was a true prince. There was only one thing wrong. This prince didn't like me. He kept looking at me like I was the place where the dog had just done his duty.

Of course, he wasn't supposed to like me in the beginning, and in the script he was bothered a lot by my lack of royal manners. But I thought his performance was missing the feeling that this prince had a little crack in him, and I might be able to reach in and touch him. No, he played it as if he was made of metal and they polished it every morning. That gave me a dull feeling. Nobody would ever believe I could make him fall in love. So I would look silly. I could give a good performance and yet it would still look like a bad performance. I always know. I can feel trouble before it has a name.

Then he'd want to rush through a scene. I'd want to slow him up, make him more human. He acted like we were all garage mechanics. The English always want everybody to be a machine anyway. That way, if you're expensive, they can put you next to another expensive machine. Also, he was used to playing the part with Vivien Leigh. She could pretend to be an American showgirl and he would probably think it was delicious. Like a husband and wife playing games in bed. He could enjoy a scene with Vivien Leigh, but not with me, the real article. All he wanted was for me to know the lines, and not be late. Get into character quickly. I felt as if he was directing me with a stopwatch. Except I liked to get to know each word. When I memorized in advance, the lines came out as if I had memorized them. An actor is best, I think, when he's like Marlon. You can hear the words coming into his head. It really feels like he hasn't already learned what he's going to say next.

Therefore I would try to slow Sir Larry up. Sometimes he would give me an instruction and I wouldn't even hear it. I'd feel like a kid in the foster home being scolded cause I didn't do the housework the way they told me. I would walk away from him then. I would say to myself, "It's my picture. It's Marilyn Monroe Productions. I hired him." I would talk to Paula. He would practically stamp his foot waiting.

"What's the key?" I would ask Paula.

"You are inviting. In this scene, the prince cannot endure how inviting you are. Marilyn, you are a ripe banana lying in a dish."

I could always play a ripe banana. I would relax even as Paula said it. Sometimes she would say, "You're a glider soaring along. You're sensitive to the wind." I would feel real alert. I might be a dumb American showgirl, but when it came to *natural* intelligence . . .

Everybody was obsessed to know what Paula was saying to me. For a tiny woman, she could look fierce. I would have loved her more except Arthur couldn't stand her, and Milton couldn't either, and I was paying her a lot of money and she didn't have the nerve to stand up to Sir Laurence Olivier. She'd waddle away when he glared.

Olivier had me very upset. I would think, "If he's such a great actor, why can't he pretend he loves me?" Then I would answer my own question: "He hates me too much to fake it." All I could see was him glaring at me. Out of his eyes came one expression: "Day after day, nothing but bloody unpreparedness."

I didn't even want to speak to Milton. He and Amy were hanging around Olivier's house as if that was the only way to get fed. Every weekend they drove over to Notley Abbey. Saturday lunch wasn't good enough, they'd spend all of Sunday there. Larry would try to get Arthur and me to come, but I wouldn't move. Acting always made me feel as if my stitches had broken loose. I just wanted Arthur to soothe me. I'd show him my lines and discuss whether they should be rewritten. Somehow Saturday and Sunday would go by and we would be into another week of shooting.

Finally we went over to visit. A lot of men and women left over from the dinner party were wearing tweed jackets. We didn't stay long. It could have been a club. Olivier took me aside and said, "Marilyn, it's going very well," which we both knew was a lie, "but I have to talk to you about the period. I think you're shuffling up the eighteenth and nineteenth centuries just a bit."

"My God," I said, "I'm trying to keep them straight."

He nodded. He looked kind for once. "The eighteenth was folly of the highest sort," he said. "People would come out with things like 'The toilette of a beautiful woman must be epic.' Why they spent lifetimes working out their bedizenments. There was virtually a philosophy of the toilette."

Arthur had come into the room, and his jaw had an expression like Larry was trying to swag the jewels. "Look," said Olivier, "today, we think of a man like Kenneth when we talk of a hairdresser. A nice man. But in that period, the eighteenth, not the period in which we're making our film, mind you, but the *eighteenth*, a coiffeur was like a gossip columnist. He could make you or he could break you. These coiffeurs were so stuffed with themselves they even took up lawsuits against wigmakers. Why, in the eighteenth century," he told Arthur and me, "women's heads were landscapes. Wooded groves. Practically had brooks running through. They even wore little sheep, with shepherds and shepherdesses. Ladies put the sun and the moon on their heads, and the planets. Some coiffeurs would actually get up on a ladder so they could manage to put their comb to the last touch on top. Then the ladies had to ride in carriages with their faces six inches from their knees." "It sounds like everybody was as uncomfortable as a movie star," I said to him. "Yes," said Olivier with a diabolical grin, "except all those grand ladies smelled. Think of it. They walked around with perfume over the body odor. An incredible time, the eighteenth. Barbaric and philosophic at once. Never confuse it, Marilyn, with our little period right here at the turn of the century, no, not the little do we're on. Our turn of the century is all hypocrisy. Everyone who wanted to, knew how to have a splendid time. Why, a man went to the ballet in order to slip away from his wife between the acts. He'd leave her in a box, nibbling away at chocolates, and mind you, the ladies brought along silver tongs so as not to get a smidgen of chocolate on those white gloves, while husband went backstage to the ballerinas in the green room. Total snobs those ballerinas. They wouldn't let a man in if he didn't belong to the Jockey Club or the Royal. Nothing but dukes."

"Plus princes?" I asked.

"Plus princes," said Olivier with a charming smile.

"I guess the fellow you play is slumming on the night he sees me."

"Of course he is, darling," said Olivier. "That's why he's so depressed. In Paris, this same fellow would be at Maxim's in the back room. In would walk a perfect tart like Cora Pearl, the most famous tart of the period. But she didn't just walk in. They brought a huge pie one night, five feet across. Who pops out of it stark naked but Cora! There wasn't a man in the room with whom she hadn't shared her carnal knowledge. Still, they took her everywhere in the daytime. A high-class tart could look awfully respectable in those days considering all those corsets and high-necked clothes. Awfully sexy clothes. That was because getting out of them was as much of a feat as breaking into a bank for the jewels. Why, a man started to breathe hard at the idea of the assault."

I nodded. I wanted to tell him that in this picture I was going to try to look like a bank that was easier than most to break into, but I could see Arthur frowning. "Isn't this picture really," he asked, "about the impact of a natural, unaffected spirit on an autocrat?"

"Yes, yes, you could say that," said Olivier, "but nonetheless, undressing a woman of the 1890's was quite the trick." "Don't we have to keep in mind," Arthur answered, "that in one way the eighteenth and nineteenth centuries were the same? There were tubercular needlewomen in both centuries. They were still sewing away with frozen fingers in unheated attic rooms."

Olivier shook his head wisely. "Arthur, there is also the idea, I must say, that the existence of aristocratic families, of *birth* itself, may be just as essential to a republic as a country's literature."

I could see Arthur wanted to go, and we left. But on the way home I kept brooding about those women who worked in unheated attic rooms. I felt I was one of them. I too was in a trap where I couldn't get out. Finally I burst into tears. When Arthur asked why, I told him I was thinking of the tubercular needlewomen he had spoken of, and he said, "Your spirit is fresh and beautiful and forever renews itself." Which is the first time he'd ever spoken to me like one of those wonderful sentences he wrote.

Then Arthur gave his broadest smile. "Listen," he said,

"I came across something funny in a book I was reading yesterday. Listen to this: 'The harsh smell of gasoline obliterates the noble smell of horse manure.' Marilyn, that's the turn of the century." I felt rosy again for the first time in a while. I wished he'd thought of the line while we were with Olivier.

Things went better with Sir Laurence for a day or two, but we got into trouble again. I just couldn't get ready with my lines. I would try to go over them with Arthur, only the lines stimulated me too much in the middle of the night. As soon as my imagination began to run, I wanted to work, and it was midnight. Then I couldn't sleep. I'd take a few pills. They would leave me stupid in the morning. It got a lot worse. My period came. I felt as if I was in contact with nothing but a headache.

There was also a new problem to contend with. Arthur didn't have much to do with his time. I began to wish he'd go teach playwriting at Oxford or something. He talked to me about revolution considerably, but sometimes I began to wonder if I was the revolution in his life. Nothing had been going right for him. I knew he hadn't written a lot since he'd known me in New York, and there were times when I worried he might be just as unhappy from the pressure as I was, except he would never show it. But he did start to visit the set every day. He was like a poor retired businessman who doesn't know what to do with himself. One time in my dressing room (it had become *our* dressing room) I asked him to look over some of my stills. That made him happy. He spent an hour with the magnifying glass. Milton came in and didn't show a thing, but I know how he felt. Stills were Milton's department.

Arthur was used to being the center of attention, but now I was. If Abraham Robert Charles happened to be right and there were two people in me, then one of us loved Arthur a lot and felt terrible that she couldn't give him more attention right now. The other person was kind of crass, however. I actually heard her voice speak in my head one day. She said, "Fuck Arthur. *I* need the attention now." It was true. I needed everything that everybody could give me. At night when I couldn't sleep, I felt as if acting was ready to kill me and death had truly slipped in. Death was a monster growing inside. It might still be tiny, but it was growing every year. Sometimes, when I couldn't sleep, I would think of Bobby de P.'s wife and wonder if I could have stood there while she was murdered. I wondered if the person in me who never got to express herself that night had anything to do with the way I felt now.

Oh, I was furious at Amy and Milton. I decided they had gone over completely to Larry Olivier's side. Amy, I knew, was disappointed in me. When we made *Bus Stop*, and went over the lines together, I had been sort of prepared. So she couldn't understand why it was different now. But I knew she blamed Arthur. Once, in desperation, he even made love to me in the dressing room as a way of trying to soothe me. Of course, that didn't work. In fact, I almost screamed at him afterward. Later, I even made the mistake of telling Amy. She didn't say a word, but I could see from her face. One of her favorite words was written all over it: appalled.

I hoped she could detect the same expression on my face the day she gave me the news that she had gone to lunch with Vivien Leigh. You wouldn't believe it, Amy informed me, they had been to see my rushes.

"What?"

Well, Vivien Leigh had said to Larry, "I want to see the rushes." Don't forget, it was once *her* part. Why, Terry Rattigan, said Amy, had even written it for her. Anyway, Vivien had said to Amy, "We'll have lunch at the studio, then look at them." I thought Amy was really very naïve under it all. She hadn't even known enough to say, "I don't want to be involved." Vivien Leigh was inviting her, so of course Amy went. Didn't have a clue that she had crossed over to the other camp.

"What did Vivien think of the rushes?" I asked.

"Well," said Amy, "she was totally amazed. The rushes were wonderful."

Even in all my bitterness, I felt a far-off happiness. "Darling," said Amy, "there you were on the screen, and here was Vivien next to me just saying quietly over and over, 'Oh, bugger all, she's very good. She's very good.' Why, you're magic, Marilyn. The minute it gets onto film, the magic occurs." I still couldn't forgive Amy. What if they hadn't liked it? What would she have thought of me then? What would she have said of me then? A friend shouldn't get into situations like that, I thought.

That same day Arthur decided to make love in the dressing room. I could practically hear the grips listening outside.

Yet all the while I had to keep consulting with everybody. I listened to what Olivier and Paula told me, what Amy had to say, what Milton proposed and Arthur suggested. It would all go round in my head like a mixer. More and more often we'd lose a day because I just felt too confused to work. In the morning the studio would be calling and Arthur'd be getting me out of bed. I'd shriek, "Why don't you stay out of this? Why don't you make *them* get me? Why don't you go and *write?*" I could see my remarks reaching into those places where Art marked things down forever. I knew he couldn't do anything about his habits. He wasn't any stronger than me. I hated him for that. Still, I'd ask his advice all over again five minutes later. I had to have him pay attention. That was like breathing to me.

Meanwhile, Arthur was getting awfully tight with a dime. It wasn't that he was thrifty, he was tight. I kept telling myself it was because he couldn't write these days. If nothing was coming in, nothing should go out. But he embarrassed me. One day Arthur wanted to buy a fishing rod and asked Milton if he could charge it to the movie company. Milton rolled his eyes. "Arthur, charge it to Marilyn Monroe Productions. I can't ask Larry to take half of this." "What are you talking about, a hundred dollars?" I asked. "Why can't Larry take half of it?" "Because that's Laurence Olivier Productions," said Milton, "and this is a fly rod for Arthur." "Just charge it to the studio," I said to Milton. "You do not understand, Marilyn," Milton said in a new ice-cold voice, "in this case, *we* are the studio. Marilyn Monroe Productions is the studio."

Olivier was rude to me right afterward. "For God's sake, Marilyn," he snapped, "be sexy." I ran right to my dressing room and phoned Lee Strasberg at his hotel in London. I said, "What's the story on being sexy, Lee? How does an actress make contact with that? Do you contact yourself?" "Marilyn," said Strasberg, "he had no right to speak to you that way." Oh, I was sick. What Olivier meant was, Go push a button in yourself. Whores can be sexy on command. I got the horrors. It brought back all of Bobby de P. Pop, I did feel sexy. I also felt more horrible than you could imagine.

The next day two other terrible things occurred. Olivier told Milton that Paula definitely must go. Final! I knew in my bones I wasn't going to be able to say no. Olivier could walk off the picture. I kept thinking of her going back to the Strasberg living room on Central Park West where they had all those wonderful shelves loaded with theater books. Her mind would be filled with theater again. But I would be alone in England.

That night, unable to sleep, I happened to see Arthur's notebook. He had left it lying wide open for me to see. On the first page he'd written that in the beginning I almost made him believe in God. I had been so beautiful and angelic. Now he had to wonder if he had set loose some kind of she-devil. If he had, it was his fault. Arthur wondered if he could look Olivier in the eye and tell him I wasn't a *troublesome bitch*. I got hysterical. I took enough sleeping pills to pass out right in the living room. I never got to work at all the next day. All the same, getting angry at Arthur, and feeling real justified about it this once, gave me a little strength. Besides, with Paula gone, Olivier was more polite. We were able to keep working on the picture day after day. But it was a very unhappy set. I went in, as Olivier would put it, unprepared. Still, I did my best. It's just that it took hours. They didn't look at the expression on my face, they studied their watches.

Arthur, meanwhile, had gotten interested in business matters. It looked as if the best way for him to snap out of a depression was to look into practical affairs. One day on the set, he said to Milton, "Maybe we can form Miller-Monroe Productions." No matter what annoyance we had with Milton, he might be doing a pretty good job as a producer. We were staying very close to budget. Arthur said that impressed him. After all, even if he didn't say it, *I* was the leading lady.

So Arthur proposed a partnership. His plays could be put into the corporation. "Taxwise," said Arthur, "it might be an asset."

Milton got a look like he was selling a carpet on the street, but you wanted to pay by check. I could see his first thought. It was: "How long since Miller has written a play?" He shook his head. "Arthur, when the film is finished, we can sit down and see if it's practical. But right now, I'm worried about the budget," said Milton. "We're slipping a little day by day."

"I don't really see your concern," said Arthur. "Warner Brothers has so much money, they won't even notice if we're ten days late."

"It's not their money," said Milton. "It's *our* money, shmuck."

Nobody spoke that way to Arthur. I saw the bones go white on the side of his jaw.

"What do you mean," I asked, " 'our money'? Warners put up the cash."

"I'm thinking of money we're hoping to make," said Milton. "Every day we lose is taken out of future profits. That's the only place our real money will be, don't you understand?"

In the old days I used to feel as strong as the entire studio every time I came late to the set. That was because it cost them money. The more they hated me, the more I knew it was costing them. I was usually so sensitive to people not liking me that tears appeared in my eyes when I was teased, yet when I was late, I could feel strong enough to let everybody hate me. I didn't care because deep down I knew they were feeling admiration. It wasn't everybody who could do that to them.

Now, due to Milton's remark, the strength was taken away from me. It was *my* money I was losing every time I was late. I couldn't stand that. When I had insomnia, I now said to myself, "This will cost a fortune tomorrow."

It was peculiar. Everything had gone wrong, especially my hope this would be a great film, and people would talk forever about Marilyn Monroe and Sir Laurence Olivier. A lot of my respect for Arthur was gone, and so was my love for Amy and Milton. I knew, somehow, that Charlie Chaplin would never make a movie with me. I didn't even trust Paula Strasberg completely. I was surrounded by people I could not trust. Suddenly I wanted to make all the money I could. Isn't that the way it always is? I guess somebody had to invent money because it's something, at least, that you can end up with.

So I started to sleep better. I was damned if I would lose

any more money. I began to listen to Olivier. He would never look like he loved me in this film, not for one moment. So what did it matter? I might as well save time. We began to move quickly. We even came in under budget. That was a record. We were the Kentucky Derby winner of budget productions. Later I heard that Jack Warner even said to Milton, "What are you handing me back $30,000 for? It'll throw out my bookkeeping."

"Take it with no complaints," said Milton.

I could have laughed, but it was too sad. Milton Greene and I were no longer speaking. He had called Arthur a shmuck, and that had been a big mistake. Arthur waited for his opportunity to reply. Just as we were finishing the film, he saw in the morning papers that Marilyn Monroe Productions had signed a deal with cameraman Jack Cardiff of *The Prince and the Showgirl* to direct a couple of properties, including Mr. Henry James's *The Turn of the Screw*. Arthur practically had me on the witness stand.

Did I know anything about this, he asked.

I started to stammer.

Well, did I? Sometimes, I said, Milton would talk to me on the set. I would hear him go over one item after another, but they would wash over. Maybe he had mentioned it. I didn't know.

Arthur pointed out that I would bring in the millions, but Milton would get half. That was bad enough, but now my future half would go out with Milton's half and be put in pictures we heard about only by reading the newspapers.

When Milton answered the phone, Arthur was already yelling so loud, Milton hung up. After that, we didn't speak. As soon as the picture was done, I even stayed up a few nights thinking of all the reasons for insomnia. We can't sleep, I decided, because we're going to lose somebody we want, or we

can't sleep because we want to kill somebody, and sometimes we can't sleep because somebody is taking our money. Of course, I also couldn't sleep because I wanted to be a lady and never make a mistake, and it seemed I never would be.

Before we left England, I was introduced to the Queen. She told me I gave a good curtsy. I explained that I had been doing a lot of practicing in my film. Princess Margaret asked if I really rode a bicycle. I started to stutter, and thought of poor Milton and said, "When I have time, I love to do it," throwing all of my personality into the remark. They looked back at me like two turnips. The test of a real lady, I decided, is that they let you do the work.

 After we got back to New York, Lee Strasberg kept saying to me, "How dare Olivier say he had a terrible time with you? You had a terrible time with him. He wasn't romantic enough." Somehow, I blamed Milton. Meanwhile, Arthur kept reminding me that until we divested ourselves of Mr. Greene, he would keep getting 49 percent of the money I made.

We called lawyers in. There were talks. Later I learned our lawyers were saying to Milton, "Mr. and Mrs. Miller feel very strongly that they do not want you to have the title of Executive Producer on *The Prince and the Showgirl*."

Milton answered, "You got to be kidding."

The negotiations dragged on for months. I found myself doing something peculiar. I would go down the block to Milton's new studio, which happened to be one street away from us, and I would say, "Listen, I really don't have anything against you, Milton, but don't you understand I have to go along? I'm married." He would look sad, and nod, and then I would go

206

away and wonder if I was one of those people who always told everybody exactly what they wanted to hear. "I love you," I would say to Milton. "Whatever happens with the lawyers, don't take it personally." Some days I would call him a lot.

Finally there was a meeting in my apartment. Our lawyer, our accountant, Milton's lawyer and Milton's accountant were present, and Arthur and Milton. I waited in the other room. I was in a bathrobe and I was crying. When our lawyer came to me, he said, "Milton Greene wants to hear you say that there will be no more Marilyn Monroe Productions." I came out and looked at Milton, and he had such a funny look, his eyes were big and brown and glistening, and he started to stutter when he saw me, and I started to stutter, and I said, "Well . . ." and burst into tears and went back into the other room. I never said it. They made the settlement. Milton finally said he'd take $100,000, no more. He did not want to make money on me. Later that night, Arthur said he had been surprised. He had thought Milton would hold out for half a million. "It was not my idea," said Milton to the newspapers, "to make money on Marilyn Monroe."

Once I met Amy on the street and my eyes got watery and we shook hands and I said, "I'm sorry," and Amy answered in her crisp little voice, "There's nothing to be sorry about," as if she was still my mother or my aunt, or certainly my big sister.

Then I ran into Milton on the street, and he said, "Things worked out that way. It's all right. I helped you, maybe you helped me, you got something you want? You're ahead? All right?"

And then I didn't run into either one of them again until I went to the opening of *The Prince and the Showgirl* at Radio City Music Hall when it came out the following summer. Amy

was very pregnant with another baby and I thought all I want more than anything in the world is a child of my own. We said hello to each other. It was like talking all the way across from one fence to the other. "Hello, how do you feel?" I asked her. "I feel fine," she said. "How are you?" "I feel fine," I said, and then I added, "You look fine." We kissed. I would even have called her up next day to ask if we could have lunch, but the reviews came for *The Prince and the Showgirl* and Bosley Crowther of *The New York Times* thought both characters were "essentially dull." I could have killed anybody in the world at that point. The *New Yorker* said, "Apart from the whimsicality of teaming up England's leading actor with a young lady whose dramatic experience has been largely confined to wiggling about in Technicolor pastries cooked up in Hollywood, it offers little in the way of diversion."

 I didn't see them for years, and all kinds of things happened to me and Arthur. I thought I was going to have a baby for a little while, but it was a tubal pregnancy. Lost. We had good times again, Art and I, but, over the whole, it got worse. By the time I made *The Misfits*, which Arthur had worked on four years, I used to shriek at him in public. Once, to my great shame, we had a big fight on the set. In front of everybody I called Arthur each and every name in the book. Then I screamed, "You even took Milton Greene away. The only man who never took advantage of me." I thought of Milton a lot after that terrible fight with Arthur. He had never become a producer again, he just kept taking photographs, and I wondered if that was out of some funny love for me, as if he wanted to say, "Hey, look, I really didn't use you. I really didn't want to. If I had used you for my own career, I could be a producer now." And I would wonder if

these words I heard Milton saying in my ear were true. I would certainly watch the magazines for his photographs, and some of them were beautiful. Oh, how exquisite he could be. My simple Milton who could never talk straight. Sometimes I would get very sad thinking of Milton. It made me miserable to look at photographs he took without me, and I would throw the magazine across the room thinking of how beautiful the young girls were now.

Once in a while, I would remember the best shooting date we ever had. It came at the end of February of 1956, just before we made *Bus Stop*. It was during that lovely winter I was living at the Waldorf. When everything, now that I look back on it, could make me feel like I was made of gold and I was always late for everything. One morning I called up Milton and said, "When are you going to take more pictures of me? Everybody takes my picture, and you're not doing it any more." Milton said, "Okay, we have a date." We set it for the morning, and I broke it because I wanted to have lunch with a friend, then I was late for a two o'clock appointment in the afternoon at his studio at 480 Lexington Avenue. It was a wonderful studio on the 11th floor, with a double ceiling and pillars, and by the time I got there, it was 5:30 in the afternoon, and dark. When I came in, he handed me a drink. I was supposed to see Arthur that evening, in fact at 6:30, but it was later than 6:30 before we even got started. By then, Milton had opened a bottle of champagne. He had no assistant with him, just the two of us, alone. There were black velvet cloths for background, and I was all in black. Amy had sent over a wonderful pair of black stockings for me with shoes attached. It was all one piece. She knew I would love it like that. Elegant in a dopey way like the guy who put the strawberry ice cream in one shoe and the vanilla in the other. I also wore a leotard for a while and a black corset, and I had black panties and a black lace top, sort of a chemise with a little openwork. After a while I even took that off. We talked and we drank and he photographed. After a while I forgot everything. Didn't think ever of what Arthur and I were supposed to do that night. Forgot it all. I was having such a good time. Milton and I lived in happiness and worked till 11 that night. I even called off the dinner with Arthur. Next day Milton called me up and said, "Holy mackerel. I think they're the best pictures I ever took."

The very last time I saw Milton was in Beverly Hills at La Scala. He was sitting at a table alone, eating, and I came over and said, "How are you?" He looked up and said, "Fine. What are you doing?" Then he asked, "Are you all right?" It was a good many months after I had gotten my divorce from Arthur Miller and I knew I looked terrible. I had too much makeup on and it was cakey. The hair was a mess. In fact, I felt horrible inside. I had been going with Frank Sinatra, but he wasn't around any more and I heard he had said, "Get rid of her." I didn't know if it was true or not, I didn't know if Sinatra would say something like that about me. I knew he would never say it to my face, but he could have said to others, "Get her away from me." Now, I sat at that table in La Scala, depressed. I wished I'd washed my face. "How are you?" I kept asking Milton. "Fine," he said, "how are you?" "All right," I said, "how's it going?" "The same," said Milton. I began to giggle. Milton would always say, "The same." He could have made a million or just lost his house, but if people asked him how he was feeling, he would always say, "The same." "How's it with you?" he asked. "Oh," I said, "it's coming along." I could see him hesitate. I know he wanted to say, "Let's go back into business again," and I wondered if I would say yes. But he didn't, and we said goodbye, and I never heard from him again until this night. It was a night in August now, in 1962, when he called me up out of nowhere and said, "Marilyn, last night Amy had a dream. In this dream, you're asking for help. She woke me up and said I should get myself on an airplane over to you because you're in trouble and you need someone." I broke down and began to cry. "Oh, Milton," I told him, "I've been having a terrible time." I explained how they'd fired me from a film and now were going to reinstate me, but my love life was a peculiar mess, and I didn't know the kind

227

of situation I was in at all, and he said, "Marilyn, do you want me to come out?" and I said, "How busy are you?" There was a pause. Milton answered, "To be perfectly honest, I'm going to Europe in a couple of days to do the collections for *Life* magazine." I said, "This is silly. My fears are silly. Go to Europe, go right ahead. Don't worry about it." Then, after we hung up, I called him back to ask if he would really come out when he was done with Paris, and we made a date to meet when he returned to America in early September. Of course, I never got to see the end of August. Or even the middle.

From the interview by Richard Meryman in *Life* magazine, August 3, 1962, published three days before Ms. Monroe's death.

When I was 11, the whole world which was always closed to me—I just felt like I was on the outside of the world—suddenly everything opened up. Even the girls paid a little attention to me because they thought, "Hmmm, she's to be dealt with!" And I had this long walk to school, 2½ miles to school, 2½ miles back—it was just sheer pleasure. Every fellow honked his horn—you know, workers driving to work, waving, you know, and I'd wave back. The world became friendly.

All the newspaper boys when they delivered the paper would come around to where I lived, and I used to hang from a limb of a tree, and I had a sort of sweatshirt on—I didn't realize the value of a sweatshirt in those days—and then I was sort of beginning to catch on, but I didn't quite get it because I couldn't really afford sweaters. But here they'd come with their bicycles, you know, and I'd get these free papers, and the family liked that, and they'd all pull their bicycles up around the tree and then I'd be hanging. I was a little shy to come down. I did get down to the curb, kinda kicking the curb, and kicking the leaves and talking, but mostly listening.

And sometimes the families used to worry cause I'd laugh so loud and so gay; I guess they felt it was hysterical. It was just all this sudden freedom because I would ask the boys, "Can I ride your bike now?" And they'd say, "Sure." Then I'd go zooming, laughing in the wind, and they'd all stand around and wait till I came back, but I loved the wind. It caressed me. . . .

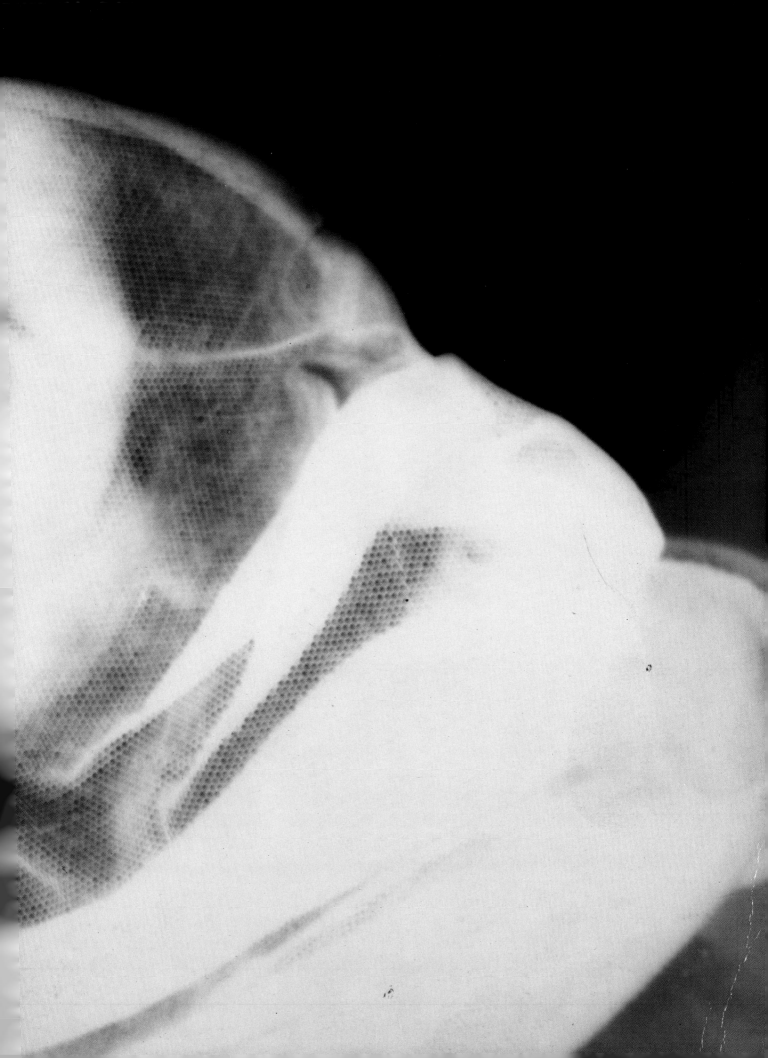

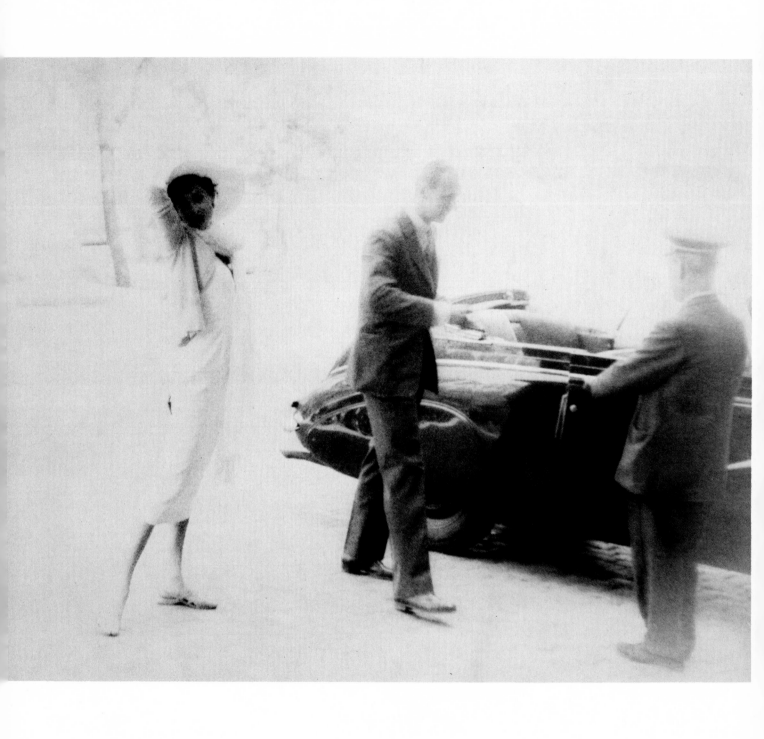

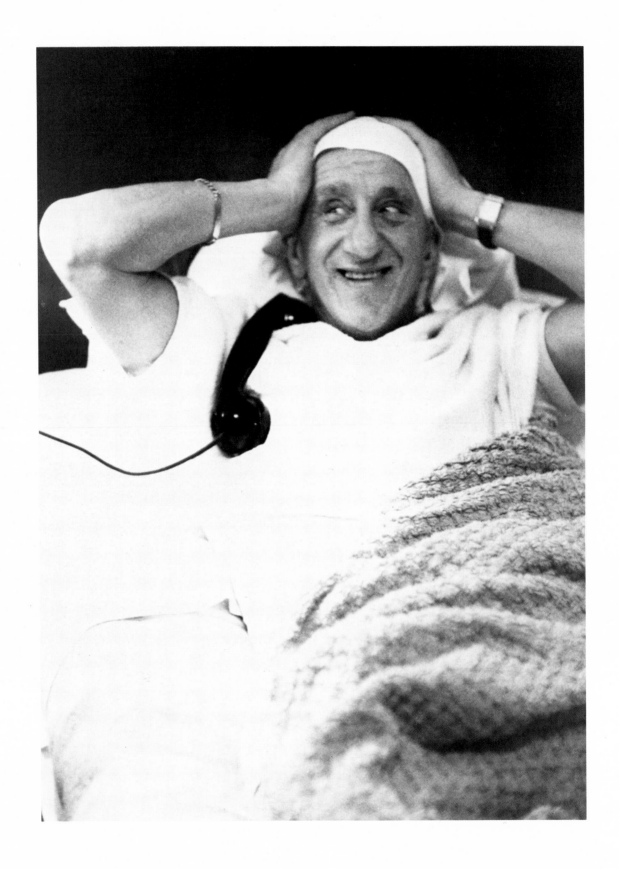

Author's Note

My last book, *The Executioner's Song*, which to many seemed a work of nonfiction, was called fiction by me, and an argument, never very interesting, went on with various critics for months. Now I face the problem of what to call this book with its splendid photographs. I am frankly at a loss. It arises from certain facts, and there are several sections within it that are all made up, and it cannot be said that the fact is wholly factual in the other places.

Perhaps we may call this an imaginary memoir, an as-told-to book, a set of interviews that never took place between Marilyn Monroe and Norman Mailer. Marilyn, it is true, did meet Milton at Twentieth Century's studios, did come to New York, did reside with Milton and Amy in Weston, Connecticut, did make the movies one has her making with the people she made them with. She even had a few of the conversations that are put in her mouth. She never did, however, write the little book this author gave her to write. On the other hand, she did read enough of Amy's books to give her a bibliography which could include *The Elegant Woman* by Gertrude Aretz and Cornelia Otis Skinner's *Demi-Castors and Grand Horizontals*, but then much of these books' agreeable material owes a debt to The Goncourt Journals.

On the other hand, Marilyn never knew anybody named Mr. Farnsworth, Miss Paisley, Rod, Rosalie, Edward, Abraham Robert Charles, or Bobby de Peralta O'Connor. It can be asked why these fictions had to be added. How can she be given a Bobby de Peralta O'Connor she never knew, and worse, a Romulus? In answer I can only plead that we cannot comprehend her inability to live with her success, or her incapacity to make movies without torturing herself and others around her, unless we are ready to posit some awful secret in her past. Doubtless she never had a relation with anyone like de Peralta O'Connor. Just as likely, she had others, maybe a dozen, maybe a hundred unrecorded episodes out of the near-anonymous years of her early career that left—we can feel it beating in her heart—some unquenchable horror, some incubus that lay over all later success.

I have to stand by my dubious method, therefore, my concoction. It has many a skew but it will insist on one virtue. The author is trying to understand his subject. If Marilyn Monroe has been treated with more intimacy than is my right, well, blame Milton's photographs. They are so resonant. They tell us so much about women in general and Marilyn in particular that I am encouraged to take these chances with my imagination. After all, the pictures speak of those little mysteries women traverse on the road to beauty, and that as we know is the beginning of all legend. Three cheers for Marilyn, then. Three for Helen of Troy.

Identifications
(Page Number & Names)